AN

UNQUIET

MIND

A MEMOIR OF MOODS AND MADNESS

Kay Redfield Jamison

WITH A NEW PREFACE BY THE AUTHOR

"An invaluable memoir of manic depression,
at once medically knowledgeable, deeply
human and beautifully written . . . at times
poetic, at times straightforward,
always unashamedly honest."
—*The New York Times Book Review*

Kay Redfield Jamison

AN UNQUIET MIND

Kay Redfield Jamison is the Dalio Family Professor in Mood Disorders and Professor of Psychiatry at the Johns Hopkins University School of Medicine. She is codirector of the Johns Hopkins Mood Disorders Center and a member of the governing board of the National Network of Depression Centers. She is also Honorary Professor of English at the University of St. Andrews in Scotland and the author of the national bestsellers *An Unquiet Mind* and *Night Falls Fast*, as well as of *Touched With Fire*, *Exuberance*, and *Nothing Was the Same*. Dr. Jamison is the coauthor of the standard medical text on bipolar illness, *Manic-Depressive Illness: Bipolar Disorders and Recurrent Depression*, and the recipient of numerous national and international literary and scientific honors, including a MacArthur Award. In 2010 she married Thomas Traill, a cardiologist and Professor of Medicine at Johns Hopkins.

People go mad in idiosyncratic ways. Perhaps it was not surprising that, as a meteorologist's daughter, I found myself, in that glorious illusion of high summer days, gliding, flying, now and again lurching through cloudbanks and ethers, past stars, and across fields of ice crystals. Even now, I can see in my mind's rather peculiar eye an extraordinary shattering and shifting of light; inconstant but ravishing colors laid out across miles of circling rings; and the almost imperceptible, somehow surprisingly pallid moons of this Catherine wheel of a planet. I remember singing "Fly me to the moons" as I swept past those of Saturn, and thinking myself terribly funny. I saw and experienced that which had been only dreams, or fitful fragments of aspiration.

Was it real? Well, of course not, not in any meaningful sense of the word real. But did it stay with me? Absolutely. Long after my psychosis cleared, and the medications took hold, it became part of what one remembers forever, surrounded by an almost Proustian melancholy. Long since that extended voyage of my mind and soul, Saturn and its icy rings took on an elegiac beauty, and I don't see Saturn's image now without feeling an acute sadness at its being so far away

AN UNQUIET MIND

Kay Redfield Jamison

VINTAGE BOOKS
A DIVISION OF RANDOM HOUSE, INC.
NEW YORK

FIRST VINTAGE BOOKS EDITION, OCTOBER 1996

Owing to limitations of space, acknowledgments for permission to
reprint previously published material may be found on page 225.

The Library of Congress has cataloged the Knopf edition as follows:
Jamison, Kay R.
An unquiet mind / Kay Redfield Jamison. — 1st ed.
p. cm.
1. Jamison, Kay R.—Mental Health. 2. Manic-depressive psychoses—
Patients—United States—Biography. 3. Women college teachers—
United States—Biography. I. Title.
RC516.J363 1995
616.89'5'0092—dc20
[B] 95-14273
CIP
Vintage ISBN: 0-679-76330-9

www.vintagebooks.com

Printed in the United States of America
50

Contents

Preface to the
Vintage Books Edition:
Fifteen Years Later

---

*F*ifteen years ago, I wrote
a book about my struggles with mania and depression,
a near-lethal suicide attempt, and a reason-defying unwillingness to take medication needed to preserve my
sanity. It was a grim book in many ways, reflecting the
grim reality of severe bipolar illness, but it was also a
book about the saving grace of love, laughter, friends
and family, as well as the healing gifts of a doctor who
practiced excellent medicine.

An Unquiet Mind was written from the heart. I had
suffered from manic-depressive (bipolar) illness from
the time I was seventeen; much later, when I finally
got treatment, I contended with the difficulties shared
by many people who have mental illness. I hoped that
writing a book about this might be of some help to
those who had experienced similar problems. Because
I also treated and studied the illness from which I suffered, I thought my account of mania and depression

might provide a somewhat different perspective on a disease that had been well-described by many, including Hippocrates five hundred years before the birth of Christ.

I did not know what the personal and professional repercussions would be once *An Unquiet Mind* was published; I did know that writing such an explicit book while also a professor of psychiatry at a prominent medical school would ratchet up the stakes by a notch or two. It did, of course, in both predictable and not-so-predictable ways.

Nothing prepared me for the number and range of responses to the publication of *An Unquiet Mind*. My colleagues at Johns Hopkins and the president of the Johns Hopkins Hospital could not have been more supportive. They unequivocally backed my decision to be public about my mental illness and many went out of their way to make it clear they thought speaking openly was exactly what needed to be done if stigmatizing attitudes were to change.

The kindness and generosity of most people was heartening, the vitriol and irrationality from others disturbing. The subject of mental illness tends to bring out a complex humanity in people; in others, it hits a deep vein of fear and prejudice. Far more people than I had realized conceptualize mental illness as a spiritual flaw or shortcoming in character. Public awareness lags behind the progress in our clinical and scientific understanding of depression and bipolar illness. It has been appalling, and at times frightening, to come face-to-face with attitudes more usually associated with the Middle Ages than with the twenty-first century.

The most lasting impressions on me after writing my book were of pain, however. Evening after evening, following my book signings, people would show me a photograph of a child, parent, or spouse who had committed suicide as a result of depression or bipolar illness. I had nearly died from suicide myself, had studied suicide and the illnesses most closely related to it for years, and had lost many friends and colleagues to it. Yet I was unprepared for the raw pain experienced by those left behind; I had not begun to fathom the sheer numbers of those devastated by the loss, guilt, and confusion that suicide generates. Prior to disclosing my own mental illness and suicide attempt, I had been on the border of this pain; now I was in the thick of it. I turned to suicide as the subject for my next book and wrote *Night Falls Fast* as a clinical *cri de coeur*. It was a difficult book to write but I could not *not* write it. The photographs of the dead would not leave my mind.

I have written several books since, each in its way about the complex and compelling nature of moods: moods that add immeasurably to life, others that cripple or destroy. *Exuberance: The Passion for Life*, which was written after *Night Falls Fast*, focused on the essential role of high energy and high enthusiasm in teaching and leadership, as well as in scientific and artistic imagination. For obvious reasons, I loved writing *Exuberance*; it was a brisk tonic that helped to offset my several-year immersion in the subject of suicide. I felt then, as I feel now, that the vitalizing moods are given short shrift compared with pathological states such as depression and anxiety.

My most recent book, *Nothing Was the Same*, was

written as a sequel to *An Unquiet Mind*. I wrote it after my husband died, when I found it hard to imagine how I would go on without him. I discovered, as many have, that there are confusing similarities, but essential differences between grief and depression. These differences are at the heart of what I wrote, a book that is first and foremost an elegy. *Nothing Was the Same* is about illness and death, love and the restorative power of grief. It is in many ways the culmination of my personal perspectives on joy, despair, and human nature. It is my favorite of the books I have written and I am glad I wrote it, but I would not want to write it again.

I feel differently about *An Unquiet Mind*. I have the occasional regret about having written it, certainly. But if, along with the writings and work of so many others, it has moved the understanding of mental illness a bit further into the light, then I am very glad that I made public my private experience of madness.

Kay Redfield Jamison, Ph.D
The Dalio Family Professor in Mood Disorders
Professor of Psychiatry
The Johns Hopkins School of Medicine
January 2011

An Unquiet Mind

Prologue

When it's two o'clock in the morning, and you're manic, even the UCLA Medical Center has a certain appeal. The hospital—ordinarily a cold clotting of uninteresting buildings—became for me, that fall morning not quite twenty years ago, a focus of my finely wired, exquisitely alert nervous system. With vibrissae twinging, antennae perked, eyes fast-forwarding and fly faceted, I took in everything around me. I was on the run. Not just on the run but fast and furious on the run, darting back and forth across the hospital parking lot trying to use up a boundless, restless, manic energy. I was running fast, but slowly going mad.

The man I was with, a colleague from the medical school, had stopped running an hour earlier and was, he said impatiently, exhausted. This, to a saner mind, would not have been surprising: the usual distinction between day and night had long since disappeared for the two of us, and the endless hours of scotch, brawling, and fallings about in laughter had taken an obvious, if not final, toll. We should have been sleeping or working, publishing not perishing, reading jour-

nals, writing in charts, or drawing tedious scientific graphs that no one would read.

Suddenly a police car pulled up. Even in my less-than-totally-lucid state of mind I could see that the officer had his hand on his gun as he got out of the car. "What in the hell are you doing running around the parking lot at this hour?" he asked. A not unreasonable question. My few remaining islets of judgment reached out to one another and linked up long enough to conclude that this particular situation was going to be hard to explain. My colleague, fortunately, was thinking far better than I was and managed to reach down into some deeply intuitive part of his own and the world's collective unconscious and said, "We're both on the faculty in the psychiatry department." The policeman looked at us, smiled, went back to his squad car, and drove away.

Being professors of psychiatry explained everything.

Within a month of signing my appointment papers to become an assistant professor of psychiatry at the University of California, Los Angeles, I was well on my way to madness; it was 1974, and I was twenty-eight years old. Within three months I was manic beyond recognition and just beginning a long, costly personal war against a medication that I would, in a few years' time, be strongly encouraging others to take. My illness, and my struggles against the drug that ultimately saved my life and restored my sanity, had been years in the making.

For as long as I can remember I was frighteningly, although often wonderfully, beholden to moods. Intensely emotional as a child, mercurial as a young girl, first severely depressed as an adolescent, and then unrelentingly caught up in the cycles of manic-depressive illness by the time I began my professional life, I became, both by necessity and intellectual inclination, a student of moods. It has been the only way I know to understand, indeed to accept, the illness I have; it also has been the only way I know to try and make a difference in the lives of others who also suffer from mood disorders. The disease that has, on several occasions, nearly killed me does kill tens of thousands of people every year: most are young, most die unnecessarily, and many are among the most imaginative and gifted that we as a society have.

The Chinese believe that before you can conquer a beast you first must make it beautiful. In some strange way, I have tried to do that with manic-depressive illness. It has been a fascinating, albeit deadly, enemy and companion; I have found it to be seductively complicated, a distillation both of what is finest in our natures, and of what is most dangerous. In order to contend with it, I first had to know it in all of its moods and infinite disguises, understand its real and imagined powers. Because my illness seemed at first simply to be an extension of myself—that is to say, of my ordinarily changeable moods, energies, and enthusiasms—I perhaps gave it at times too much quarter. And, because I thought I ought to be able to handle my increasingly violent mood swings by myself, for the first ten years I did not seek any kind of treatment. Even after my condition became a medical emergency, I still intermittently resisted the medications that both my training and clinical research expertise told me were the only sensible way to deal with the illness I had.

My manias, at least in their early and mild forms, were absolutely intoxicating states that gave rise to great personal pleasure, an incomparable flow of thoughts, and a ceaseless energy that allowed the translation of new ideas into papers and projects. Medications not only cut into these fast-flowing, high-flying times, they also brought with them seemingly intolerable side effects. It took me far too long to realize that lost years and relationships cannot be recovered, that damage done to oneself and others cannot always be put right again, and that freedom from the control imposed by medication loses its meaning when the only alternatives are death and insanity.

The war that I waged against myself is not an uncommon one. The major clinical problem in treating manic-depressive illness is not that there are not effective medications—there are—but that patients so often refuse to take them. Worse yet, because of a lack of information, poor medical advice, stigma, or fear of personal and professional reprisals, they do not seek treatment at all. Manic-depression distorts moods and thoughts, incites dreadful behaviors, destroys the basis of rational thought, and too often erodes the desire and will to live. It is an illness that is biological in its origins, yet one that feels psychological in the experience of it; an illness that is unique in conferring advantage and pleasure, yet one that brings in its wake almost unendurable suffering and, not infrequently, suicide.

I am fortunate that I have not died from my illness, fortunate in having received the best medical care available, and fortunate in having the friends, colleagues, and family that I do. Because of this, I have in turn tried, as best I could, to use my own experiences of the disease to inform my research, teaching, clinical practice, and advocacy work. Through writing and teaching I have hoped to persuade my colleagues of the paradoxical core of this quicksilver illness that can both kill and create; and, along with many others, have tried to change public attitudes about psychiatric illnesses in general and manic-depressive illness in particular. It has been difficult at times to weave together the scientific discipline of my intellectual field with the more compelling realities of my own emotional experiences. And yet it has been from this binding of raw emotion to the more distanced eye of clinical science that I feel I have obtained the freedom to live the kind of life I want, and the human experiences necessary to try and make a difference in public awareness and clinical practice.

I have had many concerns about writing a book that so explicitly describes my own attacks of mania, depression, and psychosis, as well as my problems acknowledging the need for ongoing medication. Clinicians have been, for obvious reasons of licensing and hospital privileges, reluctant to make their psychiatric problems known to others. These concerns are often well warranted. I have no idea what the long-term effects of discussing such issues so openly will be on my personal and professional life, but, whatever the consequences, they are bound to be better than continuing to be silent. I am tired of hiding, tired of misspent and knotted energies, tired of the hypocrisy, and tired of acting as though I have something to hide. One is what one is, and the dishonesty of hiding behind a degree, or a title, or any manner and collection of words, is still exactly that: dishonest. Necessary, perhaps, but dishonest. I continue to have concerns about my decision to be public about my illness, but one of the advantages of having had manic-depressive illness for more than thirty years is that very little seems insurmountably difficult. Much like crossing the Bay Bridge when there is a storm over the Chesapeake, one may be terrified to go forward, but there is no question of going back. I find myself somewhat inevitably taking a certain solace in Robert Lowell's essential question, *Yet why not say what happened?*

Part One

THE WILD BLUE
YONDER

Into the Sun

I was standing with my head back, one pigtail caught between my teeth, listening to the jet overhead. The noise was loud, unusually so, which meant that it was close. My elementary school was near Andrews Air Force Base, just outside Washington; many of us were pilots' kids, so the sound was a matter of routine. Being routine, however, didn't take away from the magic, and I instinctively looked up from the playground to wave. I knew, of course, that the pilot couldn't see me—I always knew that—just as I knew that even if he could see me the odds were that it wasn't actually my father. But it was one of those things one did, and anyway I loved any and all excuses just to stare up into the skies. My father, a career Air Force officer, was first and foremost a scientist and only secondarily a pilot. But he loved to fly, and, because he was a meteorologist, both his mind and his soul ended up being in the skies. Like my father, I looked up rather more than I looked out.

When I would say to him that the Navy and the Army were so much *older* than the Air Force, had so much more tradition and legend, he would say, Yes, that's true, but the Air Force is the *future*. Then he would always add: And—we can fly. This statement of creed would occasionally be followed by an enthusiastic rendering of the Air Force song, fragments of which remain with me to this day, nested together, somewhat improbably, with phrases from Christmas carols, early poems, and bits and pieces of the Book of Common Prayer: all having great mood and meaning from childhood, and all still retaining the power to quicken the pulses.

So I would listen and believe and, when I would hear the words "Off we go into the wild blue yonder," I would think that "wild" and "yonder" were among the most wonderful words I had ever heard; likewise, I would feel the total exhilaration of the phrase "Climbing high, into the sun" and know instinctively that I was a part of those who loved the vastness of the sky.

The noise of the jet had become louder, and I saw the other children in my second-grade class suddenly dart their heads upward. The plane was coming in very low, then it streaked past us, scarcely missing the playground. As we stood there clumped together and absolutely terrified, it flew into the trees, exploding directly in front of us. The ferocity of the crash could be felt and heard in the plane's awful impact; it also could be seen in the frightening yet terrible lingering loveliness of the flames that followed. Within minutes, it seemed, mothers were pouring onto the playground to reassure children that it was not their fathers; fortunately for my brother and sister and myself, it was not ours either. Over the next few days it became clear, from the release of the young pilot's final message to the control tower before he died, that he knew he could save his own life by bailing out. He also knew, however, that by doing so he risked that his unaccompanied plane would fall onto the playground and kill those of us who were there.

The dead pilot became a hero, transformed into a scorchingly vivid, completely impossible ideal for what was meant by the concept of duty. It was an impossible ideal, but all the more compelling and haunting because of its very unobtainability. The memory of the crash came back to me many times over the years, as a reminder both of how one aspires after and needs such ideals, and of how killingly difficult it is to achieve them. I never again looked at the sky and saw only vastness and beauty. From that afternoon on I saw that death was also and always there.

*A*lthough, like all military families, we moved a lot—by the fifth grade my older brother, sister, and I had attended four different elementary schools, and we had lived in Florida, Puerto Rico, California, Tokyo, and Washington, twice—our parents, especially my mother, kept life as secure, warm, and constant as possible. My brother was the eldest and the steadiest of the three of us children and my staunch ally, despite the three-year difference in our ages. I idolized him growing up and often trailed along after him, trying very hard to be inconspicuous, when he and his friends would wander off to play baseball or cruise the neighborhood. He was smart, fair, and self-confident, and I always felt that there was a bit of extra protection coming my way whenever he was around. My relationship with my sister, who was only thirteen months older than me, was more complicated. She was the truly beautiful one in the family, with dark hair and wonderful eyes, who from the earliest times was almost painfully aware of everything around her. She had a charismatic way, a fierce temper, very black and passing moods, and little tolerance for the conservative military lifestyle that she felt imprisoned us all. She led her own life, defiant, and broke out with abandon whenever and wherever she could. She hated high school and, when we were living in Washington, frequently skipped classes to go to the Smithsonian or the Army Medical Museum or just to smoke and drink beer with her friends.

She resented me, feeling that I was, as she mockingly put it, "the fair-haired one"—a sister, she thought, to whom friends and schoolwork came too easily—passing far too effortlessly through life, protected from reality by an absurdly optimistic view of people and life. Sandwiched between my brother, who was a natural athlete and who never seemed to see less-than-perfect marks on his college and graduate admission examinations, and me, who basically loved school and was vigorously involved in sports and friends and class activities, she stood out as the member of the family who fought back and rebelled against what she saw as a harsh and difficult world. She hated military life, hated the constant upheaval and the need to make new friends, and felt the family politeness was hypocrisy.

Perhaps because my own violent struggles with black moods did not occur until I was older, I was given a longer time to inhabit a more benign, less threatening, and, indeed to me, a quite wonderful world of high adventure. This world, I think, was one my sister had

never known. The long and important years of childhood and early adolescence were, for the most part,
very happy ones for me, and they afforded me a solid
base of warmth, friendship, and confidence. They were
to be an extremely powerful amulet, a potent and positive countervailing force against future unhappiness.
My sister had no such years, no such amulets. Not surprisingly, perhaps, when both she and I had to deal with
our respective demons, my sister saw the darkness as
being within and part of herself, the family, and the
world. I, instead, saw it as a stranger; however lodged
within my mind and soul the darkness became, it almost
always seemed an outside force that was at war with my
natural self.

My sister, like my father, could be vastly charming:
fresh, original, and devastatingly witty, she also was
blessed with an extraordinary sense of aesthetic design.
She was not an easy or untroubled person, and as she
grew older her troubles grew with her, but she had an
enormous artistic imagination and soul. She also could
break your heart and then provoke your temper beyond
any reasonable level of endurance. Still, I always felt a bit
like pieces of earth to my sister's fire and flames.

For his part, my father, when involved, was often
magically involved: ebullient, funny, curious about
almost everything, and able to describe with delight and
originality the beauties and phenomena of the natural
world. A snowflake was never just a snowflake, nor a
cloud just a cloud. They became events and characters,
and part of a lively and oddly ordered universe. When
times were good and his moods were at high tide, his
infectious enthusiasm would touch everything. Music
would fill the house, wonderful new pieces of jewelry

would appear—a moonstone ring, a delicate bracelet of cabochon rubies, a pendant fashioned from a moody sea-green stone set in a swirl of gold—and we'd all settle into our listening mode, for we knew that soon we would be hearing a very great deal about whatever new enthusiasm had taken him over. Sometimes it would be a discourse based on a passionate conviction that the future and salvation of the world was to be found in windmills; sometimes it was that the three of us children simply *had* to take Russian lessons because Russian poetry was so inexpressibly beautiful in the original.

Once, my father having read that George Bernard Shaw had left money in his will to develop a phonetic alphabet and that he had specified that *Androcles and the Lion* should be the first of his plays to be translated, we all received multiple copies of *Androcles,* as did anyone else who got in my father's flight path. Indeed, family rumor had it that almost a hundred books had been bought and distributed. There was a contagious magic to his expansiveness, which I loved, and I still smile when I remember my father reading aloud about Androcles treating the lion's wounded paw, the soldiers singing "Throw them to the lions" to the tune of "Onward, Christian Soldiers," and my father's interspersed editorial remarks about the vital—one could not stress enough *how* vital—importance of phonetic and international languages. To this day, I keep a large ceramic bumblebee in my office, and it, too, makes me laugh when I remember my father picking it up, filled to the brim with honey, and flying it through the air in various jet maneuvers including, favoritely and appropriately, a cloverleaf pattern. Naturally, when the bee was turned upside down on its flight, the honey would pour down all over the kitchen table, leaving my mother to say, "Marshall, is this *really* necessary? You're egging on the children." We would giggle approvingly, thus ensuring a few more minutes of the flight of the bumblebee.

It was enchanting, really, rather like having Mary Poppins for a father. Years later, he gave me a bracelet inscribed with words from Michael Faraday that were engraved over the physics building at UCLA: "Nothing is too wonderful to be true." Needless to say, Faraday had repeated breakdowns, and the remark is palpably untrue, but the thought and mood are lovely ones, and very much as my father could be, in his wondrous moments. My mother has said, many times, that she always felt she was in the shadow of my father's wit, charm, intensity, and imagination. Her observation that he was a Pied Piper with children certainly was borne out by his charismatic effect upon my friends and the other children in whatever neighborhood we found ourselves. My mother, however, was always the one my friends wanted to sit down and talk with: we played with my father; we talked with my mother.

Mother, who has an absolute belief that it is not the cards that one is dealt in life, it is how one plays them, is, by far, the highest card I was dealt. Kind, fair, and generous, she has the type of self-confidence that comes from having been brought up by parents who not only loved her deeply and well, but who were themselves kind, fair, and generous people. My grandfather, who died before I was born, was a college professor and physicist by training. By all accounts, he was a witty man, as well as inordinately kind to both his students and colleagues. My grandmother, whom I knew well, was a warm and caring woman who, like Mother, had a deep and genuine interest in people; this, in turn, translated into a tremendous capacity for friendship and a remarkable ability to put people at their ease. People always came first with her, as they did with my mother, and a lack of time or a busy schedule was never an excuse for being thoughtless or unavailable.

She was by no means an intellectual; unlike my grandfather, who spent his time reading, and rereading, Shakespeare and Twain, she joined clubs instead. Being both well liked and a natural organizer, she unfailingly was elected president of whatever group in which she became involved. She was disconcertingly conservative in many ways—a Republican, a Daughter of the American Revolution, and very inclined to tea parties, all of which gave my father apoplexy—but she was a gentle yet resolute woman, who wore flowered dresses, buffed her nails, set a perfect table, and smelled always of flowered soaps. She was incapable of being unkind, and she was a wonderful grandmother.

My mother—tall, thin, and pretty—was a popular student in both high school and college. Pictures in her photograph albums show an obviously happy young woman, usually surrounded by friends, playing tennis, swimming, fencing, riding horses, caught up in sorority activities, or looking slightly Gibson-girlish with a series of good-looking boyfriends. The photographs capture the extraordinary innocence of a different kind of time and world, but they were a time and a world in which my mother looked very comfortable. There were no foreboding shadows, no pensive or melancholic faces, no questions of internal darkness or instability.

Her belief that a certain predictability was something that one ought to be able to count upon must have had its roots in the utter normality of the people and events captured in these pictures, as well as in the preceding generations of her ancestors who were reliable, stable, honorable, and saw things through.

Centuries of such seeming steadiness in the genes could only very partially prepare my mother for all of the turmoil and difficulties that were to face her once she left her parents' home to begin a family of her own. But it has been precisely that persevering steadiness of my mother, her belief in seeing things through, and her great ability to love and learn, listen and change, that helped keep me alive through all of the years of pain and nightmare that were to come. She could not have known how difficult it would be to deal with madness; had no preparation for what to do with madness— none of us did—but consistent with her ability to love, and her native will, she handled it with empathy and intelligence. It never occurred to her to give up.

*B*oth my mother and father strongly encouraged my interests in writing poetry and school plays, as well as in science and medicine. Neither of them tried to limit my dreams, and they had the sense and sensitivity to tell the difference between a phase I was going through and more serious commitments. Even my phases, however, were for the most part tolerated with kindness and imagination. Being particularly given to strong and absolute passions, I was at one point desperately convinced that we had to have a sloth as a pet. My mother, who had been pushed about as far as possible by allowing me to keep dogs, cats, birds, fish, turtles, lizards, frogs, and mice, was less than wildly enthusiastic. My father convinced me to put together a detailed scientific and literary notebook about sloths. He suggested that, in addition to providing practical information about their dietary needs, living space, and veterinary requirements, I also write a series of poems about sloths and essays about what they meant to me, design a habitat for them that would work within our current house, and make detailed observations of their behavior at the zoo; if I did all this, he said, my parents would then consider finding a sloth for me.

What they both knew, I am sure, was that I was simply in love with the idea of a strange idea, and that given some other way of expressing my enthusiasms, I would be quite content. They were right, of course, and this was only further driven home by actually watching the sloths at the National Zoo. If there is anything more boring than watching a sloth—other than watching cricket, perhaps, or the House Appropriations Committee meetings on C-SPAN—I have yet to come across it. I had never been so grateful to return to the prosaic world of my dog, who, by comparison, seemed Newtonian in her complexity.

My interest in medicine, however, was lasting, and my parents fully encouraged it. When I was about twelve years old, they bought me dissecting tools, a microscope, and a copy of *Gray's Anatomy;* the latter turned out to be inordinately complicated, but its presence gave me a sense of what I imagined real Medicine to be. The Ping-Pong table in our basement was my laboratory, and I spent endless late afternoons dissecting frogs, fish, worms, and turtles; only when I moved up the evolutionary ladder in my choice of subjects and was given a fetal pig—whose tiny snout and perfect little whiskers finally did me in—was I repelled from the world of dissection. Doctors at the hospital at Andrews Air Force Base, where I volunteered as a candy striper, or nurse's aide, on weekends, gave me scalpels, hemostats, and, among other things, bottles of blood for one of my many homemade experiments. Far more important, they took me and my interests very seriously. They never tried to discourage me from becoming a doctor, even though it was an era that breathed, If woman, be a nurse. They took me on rounds with them and let me observe and even assist at minor surgical procedures. I carefully watched them take out sutures, change dressings, and do lumbar punctures. I held instruments, peered into wounds, and, on one occasion, actually removed stitches from a patient's abdominal incision.

I would arrive at the hospital early, leave late, and bring books and questions with me: What was it like to be a medical student? To deliver babies? To be around death? I must have been particularly convincing about my interest on the latter point because one of the doctors allowed me to attend part of an autopsy, which was extraordinary and horrifying. I stood at the side of the steel autopsy table, trying hard not to look at the dead child's small, naked body, but being incapable of not doing so. The smell in the room was vile and saturating, and for a long while only the sloshing of water and the quickness of the pathologist's hands were saving distractions. Eventually, in order to keep from seeing what I was seeing, I reverted back to a more cerebral, curious self, asking question after question, following each answer with yet another question. Why did the pathologist make the cuts he did? Why did he wear gloves? Where did all the body parts go? Why were some parts weighed and others not?

Initially it was a way of avoiding the awfulness of what was going on in front of me; after a while, however, curiosity became a compelling force in its own right. I focused on the questions and stopped seeing the body. As has been true a thousand times since, my curiosity and temperament had taken me to places I was not really able to handle emotionally, but the same curiosity, and the scientific side of my mind, generated enough distance and structure to allow me to manage, deflect, reflect, and move on.

When I was fifteen, I went with my fellow candy stripers on a group outing to St. Elizabeths, the federal psychiatric hospital in the District of Columbia. It was, in its own way, a far more horrifying experience than attending the autopsy. All of us were nervous during the bus ride over to the hospital, giggling and making terribly insensitive schoolgirlish remarks in a vain effort to allay our anxieties about the unknown and what we imagined to be the world of the mad. I think we were afraid of the strangeness, of possible violence, and what it would be like to see someone completely out of control. "You'll end up in St. Elizabeths" was one of our childhood taunts, and, despite the fact I had no obvious reason to believe that I was anything else but passably sane, irrational fears began to poke away at my mind. I had a terrible temper, after all, and though it rarely erupted, when it did it frightened me and anyone near its epicenter. It was the only crack, but a disturbing one, in the otherwise vacuum-sealed casing of my behavior. God only knew what ran underneath the fierce self-discipline and emotional control that had come with my upbringing. But the cracks were there, I knew it, and they frightened me.

The hospital itself was not at all the grim place I had imagined it would be: the grounds were vast, quite beautiful, and filled with magnificent old trees; at several places there were extraordinary views of the city and its rivers, and the lovely antebellum buildings conveyed the Southern graciousness that once was such an integral part of Washington. Entering the wards, however, abolished the illusion created by the genteel architecture and landscaping. There was, immediately, the dreadful reality of the sights and sounds and smells of insanity. At Andrews I was used to seeing relatively large numbers of nurses on the medical and surgical wards, but the head nurse who was taking us around explained that at St. Elizabeths there were ninety patients for each psychiatric attendant. Fascinated by the idea that one person would be expected to control so many potentially violent patients, I asked how the staff protected themselves. There were, she said, drugs that could control most of the patients, but, now and again, it became necessary to "hose them down." *"Hose them down"?!* How could anyone be so out of control that they would require such a brute method of restraint? It was something I couldn't get out of my mind.

Far worse, though, was going into the dayroom of one of the women's wards, standing dead still, and looking around me at the bizarre clothes, the odd mannerisms, the agitated pacing, strange laughter, and occasional heartbreaking screams. One woman stood like a stork, one leg tucked up; she giggled inanely to herself the whole time I was there. Another patient, who at one time must have been quite beautiful, stood in the middle of the dayroom talking to herself and braiding and unbraiding her long reddish hair. All the while, she was tracking, with her quick eyes, the movements of anyone who attempted to come anywhere near her. At first I was frightened by her, but I was also intrigued, somehow captivated. I slowly walked toward her. Finally, after standing several feet away from her for a few minutes, I gathered up my nerve to ask her why she was in the hospital. By this time I noticed out of the corner of my eye that all of the other candy stripers were huddled together, talking among themselves, at the far end of the room. I decided to stay put, however; my curiosity had made strong inroads on my fears.

The patient, in the meantime, stared through me for a very long time. Then turning sideways so she would not see me directly, she explained why she was in St. Elizabeths. Her parents, she said, had put a pinball machine inside her head when she was five years old. The red balls told her when she should laugh, the blue ones when she should be silent and keep away from other people; the green balls told her that she should start multiplying by three. Every few days a silver ball would make its way through the pins of the machine. At this point her head turned and she stared at me; I assumed she was checking to see if I was still listening. I was, of course. How could one not? The whole thing was bizarre but riveting. I asked her, What does the silver ball mean? She looked at me intently, and then everything went dead in her eyes. She stared off into space, caught up in some internal world. I never found out what the silver ball meant.

Although fascinated, I was primarily frightened by the strangeness of the patients, as well as by the perceptible level of terror in the room; even stronger than the terror, however, were the expressions of pain in the eyes of the women. Some part of me instinctively reached out, and in an odd way understood this pain, never imagining that I would someday look in the mirror and see their sadness and insanity in my own eyes.

*T*hroughout my adolescence, I was fortunate in being actively encouraged to pursue my medical and scientific interests, not just by my parents and the physicians at Andrews, but by many of my parents' friends as well. Families in the Air Weather Service tended to be posted to the same military bases, and one family in particular overlapped with ours in assignments and was especially close to us. We went on picnics together, took vacations together, shared baby-sitters, and went as a herd of ten to movies, dinners, and parties at the Officers' Club. As young children, my brother, sister, and I played hide-and-seek with their three sons; as we grew older, we went on to softball, dancing lessons, staid parties, slightly wilder parties, and then inevitably we grew up and went our separate ways. But we were almost inseparable as children in Washington and Tokyo, and then back together again in Washington. Their mother—a warm, funny, fiery, independent, practical, red-haired Irish Catholic—created a second home for me, and I would wander in and out of their house as I would our own, staying long enough to inhale pie and cookies and warmth and laughter and hours of talk. She and my mother were, and indeed still are, best friends, and I always was made to feel a part of her extended brood. She was a nurse, and she listened carefully to me as I went on at great length about my grand plans for medical school, writing, and research. Now and again she would break in with "Yes, yes, that's very interesting," "Of course you can," or "Had you thought of . . . ?" Never, but never, was there an "I don't think that's very practical" or "Why don't you just wait and see how it goes?"

Her husband, a mathematician and meteorologist, was very much the same way. He was always careful to ask me what my latest project was, what I was reading, or what kind of animal I was dissecting and why. He talked very seriously with me about science and medicine and encouraged me to go as far as I could with my plans and dreams. He, like my father, had a deep love for natural science, and he would discuss at length how physics, philosophy, and mathematics were, each in their own ways, jealous mistresses who required absolute passion and attention. It is only now, in looking back—after deflating experiences later in life when I was told either to lower my sights or to rein in my enthusiasms—that I fully appreciate the seriousness with which my ideas were taken by my parents and their friends; and it is only now that I really begin to understand how desperately important it was to both my intellectual and emotional life to have had my thoughts and enthusiasms given not only respect but active encouragement. An ardent temperament makes one very vulnerable to dreamkillers, and I was more lucky than I knew in having been brought up around enthusiasts, and lovers of enthusiasts.

So I was almost totally content: I had great friends, a full and active life of swimming, riding, softball, parties, boyfriends, summers on the Chesapeake, and all of the other beginnings of life. But there was, in the midst of all of this, a gradual awakening to the reality of what it meant to be an intense, somewhat mercurial girl in an extremely traditional and military world. Independence, temperament, and girlhood met very uneasily in the strange land of cotillion. Navy Cotillion was where officers' children were supposed to learn the fine points of manners, dancing, white gloves, and other unrealities of life. It also was where children were supposed to learn, as if the preceding fourteen or fifteen years hadn't already made it painfully clear, that generals outrank colonels who, in turn, outrank majors and captains and lieutenants, and everyone, but everyone, outranks children. Within the ranks of children, boys always outrank girls.

One way of grinding this particularly irritating pecking order into the young girls was to teach them the old and ridiculous art of curtsying. It is hard to imagine that anyone in her right mind would find curtsying an even vaguely tolerable thing to do. But having been given the benefits of a liberal education by a father with strongly nonconforming views and behaviors, it was beyond belief to me that I would seriously be expected to do this. I saw the line of crisply crinolined girls in front of me and watched each of them curtsying neatly. Sheep, I thought, Sheep. Then it was my turn. Something inside of me came to a complete boil. It was one too many times watching one too many girls being expected to acquiesce; far more infuriating, it was one too many times watching girls willingly go along with the rites of submission. I refused. A slight matter, perhaps, in any other world, but within the world of military custom and protocol—where symbols and obedience were everything, and where a child's misbehavior could jeopardize a father's chance of promotion—it was a declaration of war. Refusing to obey an adult, however absurd the request, simply wasn't done. Miss Courtnay, our dancing teacher, glared. I refused again. She was, she said, very sure that Colonel Jamison would be terribly upset by this. I was, I said, very sure that Colonel Jamison couldn't care less. I was wrong. As it turns out, Colonel Jamison did care. However ridiculous he thought it was to teach girls to curtsy to officers and their wives, he cared very much more that I had been rude to someone. I apologized, and then he and I worked on a compromise curtsy, one that involved the slightest possible bending of knees and lowering of the body. It was finely honed, and one of my father's typically ingenious solutions to an intrinsically awkward situation.

I resented the bowings, but I loved the elegance of the dress uniforms, the music and dancing, and the beauty of the cotillion evenings. However much I needed my independence, I was learning that I would always be drawn to the world of tradition as well. There was a wonderful sense of security living within this walled-off military world. Expectations were clear and excuses were few; it was a society that genuinely believed in fair play, honor, physical courage, and a willingness to die for one's country. True, it demanded a certain blind loyalty as a condition of membership, but it tolerated, because it had to, many intense and quixotic young men who were willing to take staggering risks with their lives. And it tolerated, because it had to, an even less socially disciplined group of scientists, many of whom were meteorologists, and most of whom loved the skies almost as much as the pilots did. It was a society built around a tension between romance and discipline: a complicated world of excitement, stultification, fast life, and sudden death, and it afforded a window back in time to what nineteenth-century living, at its best, and at its worst, must have been: civilized, gracious, elitist, and singularly intolerant of personal weakness. A willingness to sacrifice one's own desires was a given; self-control and restraint were assumed.

My mother once told me about a tea she had gone to at the home of my father's commanding officer. The commanding officer's wife was, like the women she had invited to tea, married to a pilot. Part of her role was to talk to the young wives about everything from matters of etiquette, such as how to give a proper dinner party, to participation in community activities on the air base. After discussing these issues for a while, she turned to the real topic at hand. Pilots, she said, should never be angry or upset when they fly. Being angry could lead to a lapse in judgment or concentration: flying accidents might happen; pilots could be killed. Pilots' wives, therefore, should never have any kind of argument with their husbands before the men leave to go flying. Composure and self-restraint were not only desirable characteristics in a woman, they were essential.

As my mother put it later, it was bad enough having to worry yourself sick every time your husband went up in an airplane; now, she was being told, she was also supposed to feel responsible if his plane crashed. Anger and discontent, lest they kill, were to be kept to oneself.

The military, even more so than the rest of society, clearly put a premium on well-behaved, genteel, and even-tempered women.

Had you told me, in those seemingly uncomplicated days of white gloves and broad-rimmed hats, that within two years I would be psychotic and want only to die, I would have laughed, wondered, and moved on. But mostly I would have laughed.

And then, in the midst of my getting used to these changes and paradoxes, and for the first time feeling firmly rooted in Washington, my father retired from the Air Force and took a job as a scientist at the Rand Corporation in California. It was 1961, I was fifteen years old, and everything in my world began to fall apart.

My first day at Pacific Palisades High School—which, par for the course for a military child, was months after the beginning of everyone else's school year—provided me with my opening clues that life was going to be terribly different. It started with the usual changing-of-the-schools ritual chant—that is, standing up in front of a classroom full of complete strangers and summing up one's life in an agonizing three minutes. This was hard enough to do in a school full of military children, but it was absolutely ridiculous in front of a group of wealthy and blasé southern Californians. As soon as I announced that my father had been an Air Force officer, I realized I could have just as easily have said he was a black-footed ferret or a Carolinian newt. There was dead silence. The only parental species recognized in Pacific Palisades were those in "the industry" (that is, in the film business), rich people, corporate attorneys, businessmen, or highly successful physicians. My understanding of the phrase "civilian school" was sharpened by the peals of laughter that followed quick on the heels of my "Yes, ma'am" and "No, sir" to the teachers.

For a long time I felt totally adrift. I missed Washington terribly. I had left behind a boyfriend, without whom I was desperately unhappy; he was blond, blue-eyed, funny, loved to dance, and we were seldom apart during the months before I left Washington. He was my introduction to independence from my family, and I believed, like most fifteen-year-olds, that our love would last forever. I also had left behind a life that had been filled with good friends, family closeness, great quantities of warmth and laughter, traditions I knew and loved, and a city that was home. More important, I had left behind a conservative military lifestyle that I had known for as long as I could remember. I had gone to nursery school, kindergarten, and most of elementary school on Air Force or Army bases; my junior and senior high schools in Maryland, while not actually on bases, were attended primarily by children from military, federal government, or diplomatic families. It was a small, warm, unthreatening, and cloistered world. California, or at least Pacific Palisades, seemed to me to be rather cold and flashy. I lost my moorings almost entirely, and despite ostensibly adjusting rapidly to a new school and acquiring new friends—both of which were made relatively easy by countless previous changes in schools that had, in turn, bred a hail-fellow-well-met sort of outgoingness—I was deeply unhappy. I spent much of my time in tears or writing letters to my boyfriend. I was furious with my father for having taken a job in California instead of staying in Washington, and I waited anxiously for telephone calls and letters from my friends. In Washington, I had been a school leader and captain of all of my teams; there had been next to no serious academic competition, and schoolwork had been dull, rote, and effortless. Palisades High School was something else entirely: the sports were different, I knew no one, and it took a very long time to reestablish myself as an athlete. More disturbing, the level of academic competition was fierce. I was behind in every subject that I had been taking, and it took forever to catch up; in fact, I don't think I ever did. On the one hand, it was exhilarating to be around so many smart and competitive students; on the other hand, it was new, humiliating, and very discouraging. It was not easy to have to acknowledge my very real limitations in background and ability. Slowly, though, I began to adjust to my new high school, narrowed the academic gap a bit, and made new friends.

However bizarre this new world seemed to me, and I to it, I actually grew to cotton to its ways. Once I got over the initial shocks, I found most of my remaining experiences in high school a remarkable sort of education. Some of it was even in the classroom. I found the highly explicit conversations of my new classmates spellbinding. Everyone seemed to have at least one, sometimes two or even three, stepparents, depending on the number of household divorces. My friends' financial resources were of astonishing proportions, and many had a familiarity with sex that was extensive enough to provide me with a very interesting groundwork. My new boyfriend, who was in college, provided the rest. He was a student at UCLA, where I worked as a volunteer on weekends in the pharmacology department. He was also everything I thought I wanted at the time: He was older, handsome, pre-med, crazy about me, had his own car, and, like my first boyfriend, loved to dance. Our relationship lasted throughout the time I was in high school, and, in looking back on it, I think it was as much a way of getting out of my house and away from the turmoil as it was any serious romantic involvement.

I also learned for the first time what a WASP was, that I was one, and that this was, on a good day, a mixed blessing. As best I could make out, having never heard the term until I arrived in California, being a WASP meant being mossbacked, lockjawed, rigid, humorless, cold, charmless, insipid, less than penetratingly bright, but otherwise—and inexplicably—to be envied. It was then, and remains, a very strange concept to me. In an immediate way all of this contributed to a certain social fragmentation within the school. One cluster, who went to the beach by day and partied by night, tended toward WASPdom; the other, slightly more casual and jaded, tended toward intellectual pursuits. I ended up drifting in and out of both worlds, for the most part comfortable in each, but for very different reasons. The WASP world provided a tenuous but important link with my past; the intellectual world, however, became the sustaining part of my existence and a strong foundation for my academic future.

*T*he past was indeed the past. The comfortable world of the military and Washington was gone: everything had changed. My brother had gone off to college before we moved to California, leaving a large hole in my security net. My relationship with my sister, always a difficult one, had become at best fractious, often adversarial, and, more usually, simply distant. She had far more trouble than I did in adjusting to California, but we never really spoke much about it. We went almost entirely our separate ways, and, for all the difference it made, we could have been living in different houses. My parents, although still living together, were essentially estranged. My mother was busy teaching, looking after all of us, and going to graduate school; my father was caught up in his scientific work. His moods still, on occasion, soared; and, when they did, the sparkle and gaiety that flew out from them created a glow, a warmth and joy that filled all of the rooms of the house. He sailed over the cusp of reason at times, and his grandiose ideas started to push the limits of what Rand could tolerate. At one point, for example, he came up with a scheme that assigned IQ scores to hundreds of individuals, most of whom were dead. The reasoning was ingenious but disturbingly idiosyncratic; it also had absolutely nothing to do with the meteorology research that he was being paid to conduct.

With his capacity for flight came grimmer moods, and the blackness of his depressions filled the air as pervasively as music did in his better periods. Within a year or so of moving to California, my father's moods were further blackening, and I felt helpless to affect them. I waited and waited for the return of the laughter and high moods and awesome enthusiasms, but, except for rare appearances, they had given way to anger, despair, and bleak emotional withdrawal. After a while, I scarcely recognized him. At times he was immobilized by depression, unable to get out of bed, and profoundly pessimistic about every aspect of his life and future. At other times, his rage and screaming would fill me with terror. I had never known my father—a soft-spoken and gentle man—to raise his voice. Now there were days, and even weeks, when I was frightened to show up for breakfast or come home from school. He also started drinking heavily, which made everything worse. My mother was as bewildered and frightened as I was, and both of us increasingly sought escape through work and friends. I spent even more time than usual with my dog; our family had adopted her as a stray puppy when we lived in Washington, and she and I went everywhere together. She slept on my bed at night and listened for hours to my tales of woe. She was, like most dogs, a good listener, and there were many nights when I would cry myself to sleep with my arms around her neck. She, my boyfriend, and my new friends made it possible for me to survive the turmoil of my home life.

I soon found out that it was not just my father who was given to black and chaotic moods. By the time I was sixteen or seventeen, it became clear that my energies and enthusiasms could be exhausting to the people around me, and after long weeks of flying high and sleeping little, my thinking would take a downward turn toward the really dark and brooding side of life. My two closest friends, both males—attractive, sardonic, and intense—were a bit inclined to the darker side as well, and we became an occasionally troubled trio, although we managed to navigate the more normal and fun-loving side of high school as well. Indeed, all of us were in various school leadership positions and very active in sports and other extracurricular activities. While living at school in these lighter lands, we wove our outside lives together in close friendship, laughter, deadly seriousness, drinking, smoking, playing truth games through the night, and engaging in passionate discussions about where our lives were going, the hows and whys of death, listening to Beethoven, Mozart, and Schumann, and vigorously debating the melancholic and existential readings—Hesse, Byron, Melville, and Hardy—we had set for ourselves. We all came by our black chaos honestly: two of us, we were to discover later, had manic-depressive illness in our immediate families; the other's mother had shot herself through the heart. We experienced together the beginnings of the pain that we each would know, later, alone. In my case, later proved rather sooner than I might have wished.

I was a senior in high school when I had my first attack of manic-depressive illness; once the siege began, I lost my mind rather rapidly. At first, everything seemed so easy. I raced about like a crazed weasel, bubbling with plans and enthusiasms, immersed in sports, and staying up all night, night after night, out with friends, reading everything that wasn't nailed down, filling manuscript books with poems and fragments of plays, and making expansive, completely unrealistic, plans for my future. The world was filled with pleasure and promise; I felt great. Not just great, I felt *really* great. I felt I could do anything, that no task was too difficult. My mind seemed clear, fabulously focused, and able to make intuitive mathematical leaps that had up to that point entirely eluded me. Indeed, they elude me still. At the time, however, not only did everything make perfect sense, but it all began to fit into a marvelous kind of cosmic relatedness. My sense of enchantment with the laws of the natural world caused me to fizz over, and I found myself buttonholing my friends to tell them how beautiful it all was. They were less than transfixed by my insights into the webbings and beauties of the universe, although considerably impressed by how exhausting it was to be around my enthusiastic ramblings: You're talking too fast, Kay. Slow down, Kay. You're wearing me out, Kay. Slow down, Kay. And those times when they didn't actually come out and say it, I still could see it in their eyes: For God's sake, Kay, slow down.

I did, finally, slow down. In fact, I came to a grinding halt. Unlike the very severe manic episodes that came a few years later and escalated wildly and psychotically out of control, this first sustained wave of mild mania was a light, lovely tincture of true mania; like hundreds of subsequent periods of high enthusiasms it was short-lived and quickly burned itself out: tiresome to my friends, perhaps; exhausting and exhilarating to me, definitely; but not disturbingly over the top. Then the bottom began to fall out of my life and mind. My thinking, far from being clearer than a crystal, was tortuous. I would read the same passage over and over again only to realize that I had no memory at all for what I just had read. Each book or poem I picked up was the same way. Incomprehensible. Nothing made sense. I could not begin to follow the material presented in my classes, and I would find myself staring out the window with no idea of what was going on around me. It was very frightening.

I was used to my mind being my best friend; of carrying on endless conversations within my head; of having a built-in source of laughter or analytic thought to rescue me from boring or painful surroundings. I counted upon my mind's acuity, interest, and loyalty as a matter of course. Now, all of a sudden, my mind had turned on me: it mocked me for my vapid enthusiasms; it laughed at all of my foolish plans; it no longer found anything interesting or enjoyable or worthwhile. It was incapable of concentrated thought and turned time and again to the subject of death: I was going to die, what difference did anything make? Life's run was only a short and meaningless one, why live? I was totally exhausted and could scarcely pull myself out of bed in the mornings. It took me twice as long to walk anywhere as it ordinarily did, and I wore the same clothes over and over again, as it was otherwise too much of an effort to make a decision about what to put on. I dreaded having to talk with people, avoided my friends whenever possible, and sat in the school library in the early mornings and late afternoons, virtually inert, with a dead heart and a brain as cold as clay.

Each day I awoke deeply tired, a feeling as foreign to my natural self as being bored or indifferent to life. Those were next. Then a gray, bleak preoccupation with death, dying, decaying, that everything was born but to die, best to die now and save the pain while waiting. I dragged exhausted mind and body around a local cemetery, ruminating about how long each of its inhabitants had lived before the final moment. I sat on the graves writing long, dreary, morbid poems, convinced that my brain and body were rotting, that everyone knew and no one would say. Laced into the exhaustion were periods of frenetic and horrible restlessness; no amount of running brought relief. For several weeks, I drank vodka in my orange juice before setting off for school in the mornings, and I thought obsessively about killing myself. It was a tribute to my ability to present an image so at variance with what I felt that few noticed I was in any way different. Certainly no one in my family did. Two friends were concerned, but I swore them to secrecy when they asked to talk with my parents. One teacher noticed, and the parent of a friend called me aside to ask if something was wrong. I lied readily: I'm fine, but thank you for asking.

I have no idea how I managed to pass as normal in school, except that other people are generally caught up in their own lives and seldom notice despair in others if those despairing make an effort to disguise the pain. I made not just an effort, but an enormous effort not to be noticed. I knew something was dreadfully wrong, but I had no idea what, and I had been brought up to believe that you kept your problems to yourself. Given that, it turned out to be unnervingly easy to keep my friends and family at psychological bay: "To be sure," wrote Hugo Wolf, "I appear at times merry and in good heart, talk, too, before others quite reasonably, and it looks as if I felt, too, God knows how well within my skin. Yet the soul maintains its deathly sleep and the heart bleeds from a thousand wounds."

It was impossible to avoid quite terrible wounds to both my mind and heart—the shock of having been so unable to understand what had been going on around me, the knowledge that my thoughts had been so completely out of my control, and the realization that I had been so depressed that I wanted only to die—and it was several months before the wounds could even begin to heal. Looking back I am amazed I survived, that I survived on my own, and that high school contained such complicated life and palpable death. I aged rapidly during those months, as one must with such loss of one's self, with such proximity to death, and such distance from shelter.

An Education for Life

I was eighteen when I reluctantly started my undergraduate studies at the University of California, Los Angeles. It was not where I wanted to go. For years I had kept in the back of my jewelry box a red-enamel-and-gold University of Chicago pin that my father had given me; it had a delicate gold chain linking the two parts of the pin, and I thought it was absolutely beautiful; I wanted to earn my right to wear it. I also wanted to go to the University of Chicago because it had a reputation for tolerating, not to say encouraging, nonconformity, and because both my father and my mother's father, a physicist, had gone there for graduate school. This was financially impossible. My father's erratic behavior had cost him his job at Rand, so, unlike most of my friends—who went off to Harvard, Stanford, or Yale—I applied to the University of California. I was bitterly disappointed; I was eager to leave California, to be on my own, and to attend a relatively small university. In the long run, however, UCLA turned out to be the best possible place for me. The University of California provided me an excellent and idiosyncratic education, an opportunity to do independent research, and the wide berth that perhaps only a large university can afford a tempestuous temperament. It could not, however, provide any meaningful protection against the terrible agitation and pain within my mind.

College, for many people I know, was the best time of their lives. This is inconceivable to me. College was, for the most part, a terrible struggle, a recurring nightmare of violent and dreadful moods spelled only now and again by weeks, sometimes months, of great fun, passion, high enthusiasms, and long runs of very hard but enjoyable work. This pattern of shifting moods and energies had a very seductive side to it, in large part because of fitful reinfusions of the intoxicating moods that I had enjoyed in high school. These were quite extraordinary, filling my brain with a cataract of ideas and more than enough energy to give me at least the illusion of carrying them out. My normal Brooks Brothers conservatism would go by the board; my hemlines would go up, my neckline down, and I would enjoy the sensuality of my youth. Almost everything was done to excess: instead of buying one Beethoven symphony, I would buy nine; instead of enrolling for five classes, I would enroll in seven; instead of buying two tickets for a concert I would buy eight or ten.

One day, during my freshman year, I was walking through the botanical gardens at UCLA, and, gazing down into the small brook that flows through the gardens, I suddenly and powerfully was reminded of a scene from Tennyson's *Idylls of the King*. Something, I think, about the Lady of the Lake. Compelled with an immediate and inflaming sense of urgency, I ran off to the bookstore to track down a copy of it, which I did. By the time I left the student union I was weighed down with at least twenty other books, some of which were related to Tennyson's poem, but others of which were only very tangentially connected, if at all, to the Arthurian legend: Malory's *Le Morte d'Arthur* and T. H. White's *The Once and Future King* were added, as were *The Golden Bough, The Celtic Realm, The Letters of Héloïse and Abelard,* books by Jung, books by Robert Graves, books about Tristan and Isolde, anthologies of creation myths, and collections of Scottish fairy tales. They all seemed very related to one another at the time. Not only did they seem related, but they seemed together to contain some essential key to the grandiosely tizzied view of the universe that my mind was beginning to spin. The Arthurian tragedy explained everything there was to know about human nature—its passions, betrayals, violence, grace, and aspirations—and my mind wove and wove, propelled by the certainty of absolute truth. Naturally, given the universality of my insights, these purchases seemed absolutely essential at the time. Indeed, they had a certain rapturous logic to them. But in the world of more prosaic realities, I could ill afford the kind of impulsive buying that this represented. I was working twenty to thirty hours a week in order to pay my way through college, and there was no margin at all for the expenses I ran up during these times of high enthusiasms. Unfortunately, the pink overdraft notices from my bank always seemed to arrive when I was in the throes of the depressions that inevitably followed my weeks of exaltation.

Much as it had during my senior year in high school, my classwork during these galvanized periods seemed very straightforward, and I found examinations, laboratory work, and papers almost absurdly easy during the weeks that the high-flying times would last. I also would become immersed in a variety of political and social causes that included everything from campus antiwar activities to slightly more idiosyncratic zealotries, such as protesting cosmetic firms that killed turtles in order to manufacture and sell beauty products. At one point I picketed a local department store with a homemade placard that showed two very badly drawn sea turtles scrunching their way across the sand, with bits of starlight overhead—a crushing reminder, I thought, of their remarkable navigational abilities—and the words YOUR SKIN HAS COST THEM THEIRS printed in large red letters beneath the picture.

But then as night inevitably goes after the day, my mood would crash, and my mind again would grind to a halt. I lost all interest in my schoolwork, friends, reading, wandering, or daydreaming. I had no idea of what was happening to me, and I would wake up in the morning with a profound sense of dread that I was going to have to somehow make it through another entire day. I would sit for hour after hour in the undergraduate library, unable to muster up enough energy to go to class. I would stare out the window, stare at my books, rearrange them, shuffle them around, leave them unopened, and think about dropping out of college. When I did go to class it was pointless. Pointless and painful. I understood very little of what was going on, and I felt as though only dying would release me from the overwhelming sense of inadequacy and blackness that surrounded me. I felt utterly alone, and watching the animated conversations between my fellow students only made me feel more so. I stopped answering the telephone and took endless hot baths in the vain hope that I might somehow escape from the deadness and dreariness.

On occasion, these periods of total despair would be made even worse by terrible agitation. My mind would race from subject to subject, but instead of being filled with the exuberant and cosmic thoughts that had been associated with earlier periods of rapid thinking, it would be drenched in awful sounds and images of decay and dying: dead bodies on the beach, charred remains of animals, toe-tagged corpses in morgues. During these agitated periods I became exceedingly restless, angry, and irritable, and the only way I could dilute the agitation was to run along the beach or pace back and forth across my room like a polar bear at the zoo. I had no idea what was going on, and I felt totally unable to ask anyone for help. It never occurred to me that I was ill; my brain just didn't put it in those terms. Finally, however, after hearing a lecture about depression in my abnormal psychology course, I went to the student health service with the intention of asking to see a psychiatrist. I got as far as the stairwell just outside the clinic but was only able to sit there, paralyzed with fear and shame, unable to go in and unable to leave. I must have sat there, head in my hands, sobbing, for more than an hour. Then I left and never went back. Eventually, the depression went away of its own accord, but only long enough for it to regroup and mobilize for the next attack.

For each awfulness in life, however, I seemed to have been given an offsetting stroke of luck. One of these occurred in my freshman year. I was taking an upper-division psychology course in personality theory, and the professor was demonstrating different ways to assess personality and cognitive structure. He held up Rorschach cards before the class and asked us to write down our responses. Years of staring up into the clouds and tracing their patterns finally paid off. My mind was flying high that day, courtesy of whatever witches' brew of neurotransmitters God had programmed into my genes, and I filled page after page with what I am sure, thinking back on it, were very strange responses. It was a large class, and everyone's answers were passed forward and handed to the professor. He read aloud from a sort of random selection; midway through I heard a recital of somewhat odd associations, and I realized to my great horror that they were mine. Some of them were humorous, but a few of them were simply bizarre. Or so they seemed to me. Most of the class was laughing, and I stared at my feet in mortification.

When the professor had finished reading my intensely scribbled sheets, he asked if the person who had written those particular responses would please stay behind to talk with him for a while. I was convinced that, being a psychologist, he could see straight into my psychotic underpinnings. I was terrified. Looking back on it, what I suspect he actually saw was someone who was very intense, quite determined, serious, and probably rather troubled. At the time, being acutely aware of just how disturbed I really was, I assumed that the extent of my problems was equally obvious to him. He asked me to walk back to his office with him, and, while I was conjuring up images of being admitted to a psychiatric ward, he said that in all of his years of teaching he had never encountered such "imaginative" responses to the Rorschach. He was kind enough to call creative that which some, no doubt, would have called psychotic. It was my first lesson in appreciating the complicated, permeable boundaries between bizarre and original thought, and I remain deeply indebted to him for the intellectual tolerance that cast a positive rather than pathological hue over what I had written.

The professor asked me about my background, and I explained that I was a freshman, wanted to become a doctor, and that I was working my way through school. He pointed out the university regulations stating that I was not allowed to be taking his course, as it was for juniors and seniors only, and I said that I knew that, but it looked interesting and the rule seemed completely arbitrary. He laughed out loud, and I suddenly realized that I was finally in a situation where someone actually respected my independence. This was not Miss Courtnay, and I was not expected to curtsy. He said he had a position on his grant for a lab assistant and asked me if I would be interested. I was more than interested. It meant that I could give up my unremittingly boring job as a cashier in a women's clothing store and that I could learn to do research.

It was a wonderful experience: I learned to code and analyze data, program computers, review the research literature, design studies, and write up scientific papers for publication. The professor I was working with was studying the structure of human personality, and I found the idea of investigating individual differences among people absolutely fascinating. I immersed myself in the work and found it not only a source of education and income, but escape as well. Unlike attendance at classes—which seemed stifling and, like the rest of the world's schedules, based on an assumption of steadiness and consistency in moods and performance—the research life allowed an independence and flexibility of schedule that I found exhilarating. University administrators do not consider the pronounced seasonal changes in behaviors and abilities that are part and parcel of the lives of most manic-depressives. My undergraduate transcript, consequently, was riddled with failing grades and incompleted classes, but my research papers, fortunately, offset my often dreary grades. My mercurial moods and recurrent, very black depressions took a huge personal and academic toll during those college years.

At the age of twenty, after two years of undergraduate studies, I took off a year from the turmoil that had become my life to study at the University of St. Andrews in Scotland. My brother and cousin were studying at English universities at the time, and they suggested that I come over and join them. But I had been deeply affected by the Scottish music and poetry that my father loved, and there was something very appealing to me in the Celtic melancholy and fire that I associated with the Scottish side of my ancestry, even though I at the same time wanted to get away from my father's black, unpredictable moods. Not entirely away, however; I think I had a vague notion that I might better understand my own chaotic feelings and thinking if I returned in some sense to the source. I applied for a federal grant, which enabled me for the first time to become a full-time student, and I left Los Angeles for a year of science by day, and music and poetry by night.

St. Andrews, my tutor was saying, was the only place he knew where it snowed horizontally. An eminent neurophysiologist, he was a tall, lanky, and droll Yorkshireman who, like many of his fellow English, believed that rather superior weather, to say nothing of civilization, ended where the Scottish countryside began. He had a point about the weather. The ancient, gray-stoned town of St. Andrews sits right on the North Sea and takes blasts of late-autumn and winter winds that have to be experienced to be believed. I had been living in Scotland for several months by that time, and I had become a definite believer. The winds were especially harsh just off the town's East Sands, where the university's marine biology laboratory had been built.

There were ten or so of us third-year zoology students, and we were sitting, shivering, wool layered, wool gloved, and teeth chattering, in the damp cold of the tank-filled laboratory. My tutor seemed even more puzzled by my being in these advanced zoology courses than I was. He was an authority on what one might have thought was a somewhat specialized portion of the animal kingdom, namely the auditory nerve of the locust, and just prior to his remarks about horizontal snowfalls in Scotland he had put my striking ignorance of zoological matters out into the public domain.

The task at hand was to set up electrophysiological recordings from the locust's auditory nerve; the rest of the students—all of whom had been specializing in science for many years—had already, and neatly, dissected out the necessary tidbits of bug and were duly recording away. I hadn't any idea what I was doing, my tutor knew this, and I was wondering yet again why the university had placed me at this level of science studies. I had gotten as far as picking out the locust from his cage—because it was kept warm, I prolonged my stay in the insect room for a rather lingering time—and had finally narrowed down its body regions into wings, body, and head. This was not going to get me very far. I felt my tutor's tall presence behind me and turned to see a sardonic smile on his face. He went to the chalkboard, drew what certainly looked to be a locust, circled a region on the animal's head, and said in his most elaborate accent, "For your edification, Miss Jamison, he-ah is the e-ah"; the class roared, so did I, and I reconciled myself to a year of being truly and hopelessly behind— I was; but I learned a lot, and had great fun as I did so. (My laboratory notes for the locust experiment reflect my early recognition that I was in over my head; after detailing the experimental method in my lab report— "The head, wings, and legs were removed from a locust. After exposing the air sacs by cutting the metathoracic sternites, the auditory nerve was located and cut centrally to exclude the possibility of responses from the cerebral ganglion," and so on—the write-up ended with "Due to a misunderstanding of instructions, and a general lack of knowledge about what was going on, a broader range of pitch stimulation was not tested and, by the time the misunderstanding was understood, the auditory nerve was fatigued. So was I.")

There were, however, definite advantages to studying invertebrate zoology. For starters, unlike in psychology, you could eat your subjects. The lobsters—fresh from the sea and delicious—were especially popular. We cooked them in beakers over Bunsen burners until one of our lecturers, remarking that "It has not gone unnoticed that some of your subjects seem to be letting themselves out of their tanks at night," put a halt to our attempts to supplement college meals.

That year I walked for long hours along the sea and through the town and sat for hours mulling and writing among the ancient ruins of the city. I never tired of imagining what the twelfth-century cathedral must once have been, what glorious stained glass must once have filled its now-empty stone-edged windows; nor could I escape the almost archetypal pullings of Sunday services in the college chapel, which, like the university itself, had been built during the early fifteenth century. The medieval traditions of learning and religion were threaded together in a deeply mystifying and wonderful way. The thick scarlet gowns of the undergraduates, said to be brightly colored because of an early Scottish king's decree that students, as potentially dangerous to the State, should be easily recognized, brought vivid contrast to the gray buildings of the town; and, after chapel, the red-gowned students would walk to the end of the town's pier, further extending their vivid contrast to the dark skies and the sea.

It was, it is, a mystical place: full of memories of cold, clear nights and men and women in evening dress, long gloves, silk scarves, kilts, and tartan sashes over the shoulders of women in elegant floor-length silk gowns; an endless round of formal balls; late dinner parties of salmon, hams, fresh game, sherry, malt whiskies, and port; bright scarlet gowns on the backs of students on bicycles, in dining and lecture halls, in gardens, and on the ground as picnic blankets in the spring. There were late nights of singing and talking with my Scottish roommates; long banks of daffodils and bluebells on the hills above the sea; seaweed and rocks and limpet shells along the yellow, high-tided sands, and ravishingly beautiful Christmas services at the end of term: undergraduates in their long, bright gowns of red, and graduate students in their short, black somber ones; the old and beautiful carols; hanging lamps of gold-chained crowns, and deeply carved wooden choir stalls; the recitation of lessons in both the English public school and the far gentler, more lyrical Scottish accents. Leaving the chapel late that winter night was to enter onto an ancient scene, the sight of scarlet against snow, the ringing of bells, and a clear, full moon.

St. Andrews provided a gentle forgetfulness over the preceding painful years of my life. It remains a haunting and lovely time to me, a marrow experience. For one who during her undergraduate years was trying to escape an inexplicable weariness and despair, St. Andrews was an amulet against all manner of longing and loss, a year of gravely held but joyous remembrances. Throughout and beyond a long North Sea winter, it was the Indian summer of my life.

I was twenty-one years old when I left Scotland and returned to UCLA. It was an abrupt shift in mood and surroundings, and an even more abrupt disruption to the pace of my life. I tried to settle back into my old world and routines but found it difficult to do so. For a year I had been free of having to work twenty or thirty hours a week in order to support myself, but now I once again had to juggle my work, classes, social life, and disruptive moods. My career plans also had changed. It had become clear to me over time that my mercurial temperament and physical restlessness were going to make medical school—especially the first two years, which required sitting still in lecture halls for hours at a time—an unlikely proposition. I found it difficult to stay put for long and found that I learned best on my own. I loved research and writing, and the thought of being chained to the kind of schedule that medical school required was increasingly repugnant. As important, I had read William James's great psychological study, *The Varieties of Religious Experience,* during my year in St. Andrews and had become completely captivated by the idea of studying psychology, especially individual differences in temperament and variations in emotional capacities, such as mood and intense perceptions. I also had begun working with a second professor on his research grant, a fascinating study of the psychological and physiological effects of mood-altering drugs such as LSD, marijuana, cocaine, opiates, barbiturates, and amphetamines. He was particularly interested in why some individuals were drawn to one class of drugs, for example, the hallucinogens, while others gravitated toward drugs that dampened or elevated mood. He, like me, was intrigued by moods.

This professor—a tall, shy, brilliant man—was himself inclined to quick and profound mood swings. I found working for him, first as a research assistant and then as a doctoral student, an extraordinary experience: he was immensely creative, curious, and open-minded; difficult but fair in his intellectual demands; and exceptionally kind in understanding my own fluctuating moods and attentiveness. We had a kind of intuition about one another that was, for the most part, left unsaid, although occasionally one or the other of us would bring up the subject of black moods. My office was adjacent to his, and he would, during my depressed times, ask about how I was feeling, comment that I looked tired or pensive or discouraged, and ask what he could do to help.

One day in our discussions we found out that each of us had been rating our own moods—he on a 10-point scale of subjective ratings ranging from "terrible" to "great," and me on a scale ranging from −3 (paralytic and entirely despairing) to +3 (magnificent mood and vitality), in an attempt to discover some sort of rhyme or reason to their comings and goings. Now and again we would talk about the possibility of taking antidepressant medications, but we were deeply skeptical that they would work and wary of potential side effects. Somehow, like so many people who get depressed, we felt our depressions were more complicated and existentially based than they actually were. Antidepressants might be indicated for psychiatric patients, for those of weaker stock, but not for us. It was a costly attitude; our upbringing and pride held us hostage. Despite my swings in mood—for my depressions continued to be preceded by giddy, intoxicating highs—I felt I had a haven in my undergraduate research assistantship with him. Many times, having turned out the light in my office in order to sleep because I couldn't face the world, I would wake up to find his coat over my shoulders and a note on top of my computer printout saying "You'll feel better soon."

My tremendous enjoyment of and education from the work I was doing with him, the continued satisfaction in my other work with the more mathematically inclined professor with whom I had been working since my freshman year, the strong influence of William James, and the instability and restlessness of my temperament all combined to help me make up my mind to study for a Ph.D. in psychology rather than go to medical school. UCLA was then, and still is, one of the best graduate programs in psychology in the United States; I applied for admission and began my doctoral studies in 1971.

I decided early in graduate school that I needed to do something about my moods. It quickly came down to a choice between seeing a psychiatrist or buying a horse. Since almost everyone I knew was seeing a psychiatrist, and since I had an absolute belief that I should be able to handle my own problems, I naturally bought a horse. Not just any horse, but an unrelentingly stubborn and blindingly neurotic one, a sort of equine Woody Allen, but without the entertainment value. I had imagined, of course, a *My Friend Flicka* scenario: my horse would see me in the distance, wiggle his ears in eager anticipation, whinny with pleasure, canter up to my side, and nuzzle my breeches for sugar or carrots. What I got instead was a wildly anxious, frequently lame, and not terribly bright creature who was terrified of snakes, people, lizards, dogs, and other horses—in short, terrified of anything that he might reasonably be expected to encounter in life— thus causing him to rear up on his hind legs and bolt madly about in completely random directions. In the clouds-and-silver-linings department, however, whenever I rode him I was generally too terrified to be depressed, and when I was manic I had no judgment anyway, so maniacal riding was well suited to the mood.

Unfortunately, it was not only a crazy decision to buy a horse, it was also stupid. I may as well have saved myself the trouble of cashing my Public Health Service fellowship checks, and fed him the checks directly: besides shoeing him and boarding him—with veterinary requirements that he supplement his regular diet with a kind of horsey granola that cost more than a good pear brandy—I also had to buy him special orthopedic shoes to correct, or occasionally correct, his ongoing problems with lameness. These shoes left Gucci and Neiman-Marcus in the dust, and, after a painfully acquired but profound understanding of why people shoot horse traders, and horses, I had to acknowledge that I was a graduate student, not Dr. Dolittle; more to the point, I was neither a Mellon nor a Rockefeller. I sold my horse, as one passes along the queen of spades, and started showing up for my classes at UCLA.

Graduate school was the fun I missed as an undergraduate. It was a continuation, in some respects, of the Indian summer I enjoyed in St. Andrews. Looking back over those years with the cool clinical perspective acquired much later, I realize that I was experiencing what is so coldly and prosaically known as a remission—common in the early years of manic-depressive illness and a deceptive respite from the savagely recurrent course that the untreated illness ultimately takes— but I assumed I was just back to my normal self. In those days there were no words or disease names or concepts that could give meaning to the awful swings in mood that I had known.

Graduate school was not only relative freedom for me from my illness, but it was also freedom from the highly structured existence of undergraduate studies. Although I skipped more than half of my formal lectures, it didn't really matter; as long as one ultimately performed, the erratic ways that one took to get there were considerably less important. I was married, too, by this point, to a French artist who not only was a talented painter but an exceedingly kind and gentle person. He and I had met in the early seventies, at a brunch given by mutual friends. It was a time of long hair, social unrest, graduate school deferments, and Vietnam War protests, and I was relieved to find someone who was, for a switch, essentially apolitical, highly intelligent but unintellectual, and deeply committed to the arts. We were very different, but we liked one another immediately; we found out quickly that we shared a passionate love for painting, music, and the natural world. I was, at the time, painfully intense, rail thin, and, when not moribund, filled to the brim with a desire for an exciting life, a high-voltage academic career, and a pack of children. Photographs from that time show a tall, extraordinarily handsome, dark-haired, gentle, and brown-eyed man who, while consistent in his own appearance, is accompanied by a wildly variable woman in her midtwenties: in one picture laughing, in a floppy hat, with long hair flying; in another pensive, brooding, looking infinitely older, far more soberly and boringly dressed. My hair, like my moods, went up and down: long for a time, until an I-look-like-a-toad mood would sweep over me; thinking a radical change might help, I then would have it cut to a bob. The moods, the hair, the clothes all changed from week to week, month to month. My husband, on the other hand, was steady, and in most ways we ended up complementing one another's temperaments.

Within months of our meeting we were living together in a small apartment near the ocean. It was a quiet, normal sort of existence, filled with movies, friends, and trips to Big Sur, San Francisco, and Yosemite. The safety of our marriage, the closeness of good friends, and the intellectual latitude provided by graduate school were very powerful in providing a reasonably quiet and harbored world.

I had started off studying experimental psychology, especially the more physiological and mathematical sides of the field, but after several months of clinical studies at the Maudsley Hospital in London—which I had completed just prior to meeting my husband—I decided to switch to clinical psychology. I had an increasing personal, as well as professional, interest in the field. My course work, which had focused on statistical methods, biology, and experimental psychology, now switched to psychopharmacology, psychopathology, clinical methods, and psychotherapy. Psychopathology—the scientific study of mental disorders—proved enormously interesting, and I found that seeing patients was not only fascinating but intellectually and personally demanding. Despite the fact that we were being taught how to make clinical diagnoses, I still did not make any connection in my own mind between the problems I had experienced and what was described as manic-depressive illness in the textbooks. In a strange reversal of medical-student syndrome, where students become convinced that they have whatever disease it is they are studying, I blithely went on with my clinical training and never put my mood swings into any medical context whatsoever. When I look back on it, my denial and ignorance seem virtually incomprehensible. I noticed, though, that I was more comfortable treating psychotic patients than were many of my colleagues.

At that time, in clinical psychology and psychiatric residency programs, psychosis was far more linked to schizophrenia than manic-depressive illness, and I learned very little about mood disorders in any formal sense. Psychoanalytic theories still predominated. So for the first two years of treating patients, I was supervised almost entirely by psychoanalysts; the emphasis in treatment was on understanding early experiences and conflicts; dreams and symbols, and their interpretation, formed the core of psychotherapeutic work. A more medical approach to psychopathology—one that centered on diagnosis, symptoms, illness, and medical treatments—came only after I started my internship at the UCLA Neuropsychiatric Institute. Although I have had many disagreements with psychoanalysts over the years—and particularly virulent ones with those analysts who oppose treating severe mood disorders with medications, long after the evidence clearly showed that lithium and the antidepressants are far more effective than psychotherapy alone—I have found invaluable the emphasis in my early psychotherapy training on many aspects of psychoanalytic thought. I shed much of the psychoanalytic language as time went by, but the education was an interesting one, and I've never been able to fathom the often unnecessarily arbitrary distinctions between "biological" psychiatry, which emphasizes medical causes and treatments of mental illness, and the "dynamic" psychologies, which focus more on early developmental issues, personality structure, conflict and motivation, and unconscious thought.

Extremes, however, are always absurd, and I found myself amazed at the ridiculous level to which uncritical thought can sink. At one point in our training we were expected to learn how to administer various psychological tests, including intelligence tests such as the Wechsler Adult Intelligence Scale, or WAIS, and personality tests such as the Rorschach. My first practice subject was my husband, who, as an artist, not surprisingly scored off the top on the visual performance parts of the WAIS, frequently having to explain to me how to put the block designs together. His Rorschach responses were of a level of originality that I have not seen since. On the Draw-A-Person test I noticed that he seemed to be taking it very seriously, drawing meticulously and slowly what I assumed would be some kind of revealing self-portrait. When he finally showed the picture to me, however, it was a wonderfully elaborated orangutan whose long arms extended along the borders of the page.

I thought it was marvelous and took the results of his WAIS, Rorschach, and Draw-A-Person to my psychological-testing supervisor. She was an entirely humorless and doctrinaire psychoanalyst who spent more than an hour interpreting, in the most fatuous and speculative manner, the primitive and repressed rage of my husband, his intrapsychic conflicts, his ambivalences, his antisocial nature, and his deeply disturbed personality structure. My now former husband, whom I have never, in almost twenty-five years, known to lie, was being labeled a sociopath; a man who was quite singularly straightforward and gentle was interpreted as deeply disturbed, conflicted, and filled with rage. All because he had done something different on a test. It was absurd. Indeed, it was so ridiculous to me that, after having giggled uncontrollably for quite a long while, thus provoking even further wrath—and, worse yet, further interpretations—I half stormed, half laughed my way out of her office and refused to write up the test report. This, too, needless to say, was obsessed over, dissected, and analyzed.

Most of my real education came from the wide variety and large number of patients that I evaluated and treated during my predoctoral clinical internships. Along the way, I completed the course work for my two minor fields, psychopharmacology and animal behavior. I particularly loved studying animal behavior and supplemented the courses offered by the psychology department with graduate courses given by the zoology department. These zoology courses focused on the biology of aquatic mammals and covered not only the biology and natural history of sea otters, seals, sea lions, whales, and dolphins, but also such esoterica as the cardiovascular adaptations made to diving by sea lions and whales and the communication systems used by dolphins. It was learning for learning's sake, and I loved it. None of this had any relevance whatsoever to anything else I was studying or doing, nor to anything I have done since, but they were far and away the most interesting classes I took in graduate school.

Qualifying examinations came and went; I conducted a completely uninspired doctoral study about heroin addiction and wrote a correspondingly uninspired dissertation based upon it; then after two weeks of frantically cramming every bit of trivia that I could into my brain, I walked into a room filled with five unsmiling men seated around a table, sat down, and went through the ordeal that is politely known as a Final Oral Examination, or, more aptly, in a military sense, the defense of one's dissertation. Two of the men at the table were the professors with whom I had worked for years; one of them was easy on me, the other was—I suppose in an attempt to demonstrate impartiality—unrelenting. One of the three psycho-pharmacologists, the only one without tenure, felt compelled to give me a particularly bad time, but the other two, who were full professors, clearly felt he had gone too far in establishing his mastery of the minutia of statistics and research design and eventually forced him to return to a less Rottweilerian level of general civility. After three hours of the intricate intellectual ballet that constituted the defense of my thesis, I left the room and stood in the hallway while they voted; endured the requisite moments of agony; and returned to find the same five men who, hours earlier, had seemed so grim and unfriendly. But this time they were smiling; their hands were outstretched to shake mine; and they all said, to my vast relief and pleasure, Con-gratulations.

The rites of passage in the academic world are arcane and, in their own way, highly romantic, and the tensions and unpleasantries of dissertations and final oral ex-aminations are quickly forgotten in the wonderful moments of the sherry afterward, admission into a very old club, parties of celebration, doctoral gowns, aca-demic rituals, and hearing for the first time "Dr.," rather than "Miss," Jamison. I was hired as an assistant professor in the UCLA Department of Psychiatry, got good parking for the first time in my life, joined the faculty club posthaste, and began to work my way up the academic food chain. I had a glorious—as it turns out, too glorious—summer, and, within three months of becoming a professor, I was ravingly psychotic.

Part Two

A NOT SO FINE MADNESS

Flights of the Mind

*T*here *is a particular kind of
pain, elation, loneliness, and terror involved in this kind of
madness. When you're high it's tremendous. The ideas and
feelings are fast and frequent like shooting stars, and you follow them until you find better and brighter ones. Shyness
goes, the right words and gestures are suddenly there, the
power to captivate others a felt certainty. There are interests
found in uninteresting people. Sensuality is pervasive and
the desire to seduce and be seduced irresistible. Feelings of
ease, intensity, power, well-being, financial omnipotence, and
euphoria pervade one's marrow. But, somewhere, this
changes. The fast ideas are far too fast, and there are far too
many; overwhelming confusion replaces clarity. Memory
goes. Humor and absorption on friends' faces are replaced by
fear and concern. Everything previously moving with the
grain is now against—you are irritable, angry, frightened,
uncontrollable, and enmeshed totally in the blackest caves of
the mind. You never knew those caves were there. It will
never end, for madness carves its own reality.*

It goes on and on, and finally there are only others' rec-
ollections of your behavior—your bizarre, frenetic, aimless
behaviors—for mania has at least some grace in partially
obliterating memories. What then, after the medications, psy-
chiatrist, despair, depression, and overdose? All those incred-
ible feelings to sort through. Who is being too polite to say
what? Who knows what? What did I do? Why? And most
hauntingly, when will it happen again? Then, too, are the
bitter reminders—medicine to take, resent, forget, take,
resent, and forget, but always to take. Credit cards revoked,
bounced checks to cover, explanations due at work, apologies
to make, intermittent memories (what did I do?), friend-
ships gone or drained, a ruined marriage. And always, when
will it happen again? Which of my feelings are real? Which
of the me's is me? The wild, impulsive, chaotic, energetic,
and crazy one? Or the shy, withdrawn, desperate, suicidal,
doomed, and tired one? Probably a bit of both, hopefully
much that is neither. Virginia Woolf, in her dives and climbs,
said it all: "How far do our feelings take their colour from
the dive underground? I mean, what is the reality of any
feeling?"

I did not wake up one day
to find myself mad. Life should be so simple. Rather, I
gradually became aware that my life and mind were
going at an ever faster and faster clip until finally, over
the course of my first summer on the faculty, they both
had spun wildly and absolutely out of control. But the
acceleration from quick thought to chaos was a slow
and beautifully seductive one. In the beginning, everything seemed perfectly normal. I joined the psychiatry
faculty in July of 1974 and was assigned to one of the

adult inpatient wards for my clinical and teaching responsibilities. I was expected to supervise psychiatric residents and clinical psychology interns in diagnostic techniques, psychological testing, psychotherapy, and, because of my background in psychopharmacology, some issues related to drug trials and medications. I was also the faculty liaison between the Departments of Psychiatry and Anesthesiology, where I did consultations, seminars, and put into place some research protocols that were designed to investigate psychological and medical aspects of pain. My own research consisted primarily of writing up some of the drug studies I had carried out in graduate school. I had no particular interest in either clinical work or research related to mood disorders, and as I had been almost entirely free of serious mood swings for more than a year, I assumed that those problems were behind me. Feeling normal for any extended period of time raises hopes that turn out, almost invariably, to be writ on water.

I settled into my new job with great optimism and energy. I enjoyed teaching, and, although it initially seemed strange to be supervising the clinical work of others, I liked it. I found the transition from intern to faculty status far less difficult than I had imagined; it was, needless to say, one that was greatly helped along by an invigorating difference in salary. The relative freedom I had to pursue my own academic interests was intoxicating. I worked very hard and, looking back on it, slept very little. Decreased sleep is both a symptom of mania and a cause, but I didn't know that at the time, and it probably would not have made any difference to me if I had. Summer had often brought me longer nights and higher moods, but this time it pushed me into far higher, more dangerous and psychotic places than I had ever been. Summer, a lack of sleep, a deluge of work, and exquisitely vulnerable genes eventually took me to the back of beyond, past my familiar levels of exuberance and into florid madness.

*T*he chancellor's garden party was given annually to welcome new faculty members to UCLA. By coincidence the man who was to become my psychiatrist also happened to be attending the garden party, having himself just joined the adjunct medical school faculty. It proved to be an interesting example of the divide between one's self-perception and the cooler, more measured observations of an experienced clinician who suddenly found himself in a social situation watching a somewhat wild-eyed and frenzied former intern that he, as the recent chief resident, had supervised the preceding year. My recollection of the situation was that I was perhaps a bit high, but primarily I remember talking to scads of people, feeling that I was irresistibly charming, and zipping around from hors d'oeuvre to hors d'oeuvre, and drink to drink. I talked with the chancellor for a long time; he, of course, had absolutely no idea who I was, but he was either being exceedingly polite by talking to me for so long or simply holding true to his reputation as having a penchant for young women. Whatever he actually felt, I was sure he was finding me captivating.

I also had an extended and rather odd conversation with the chairman of my department—odd, but a conversation I found delightful. My chairman was himself a not unexpansive person, and he harbored a very imaginative mind that did not always keep within the common grazing lands of academic medicine. He was somewhat notorious within psychopharmacology circles for having accidentally killed a rented circus elephant with LSD—a complicated, rather improbable story involving large land mammals in must, temporal lobe glands, the effects of hallucinogenic drugs on violent behavior, and miscalculated volumes and surface areas—and we started a long, dendritic discussion about doing research on elephants and hyraxes. Hyraxes are small African animals that bear no resemblance whatsoever to elephants but, based on the patterning of their teeth, are thought to be their closest living relatives. I cannot begin to remember the detailed arguments and common interests underlying this strange and extremely animated conversation—except that I immediately, and with great gusto, took upon myself the task of tracking down every article, and there were hundreds, ever written about hyraxes. I also volunteered to work on animal behavior studies at the Los Angeles Zoo, as well as to co-teach a course in ethology and yet another one in pharmacology and ethology.

My memories of the garden party were that I had had a fabulous, bubbly, seductive, assured time. My psychiatrist, however, in talking with me about it much later, recollected it very differently. I was, he said, dressed in a remarkably provocative way, totally unlike the conservative manner in which he had seen me dressed over the preceding year. I had on much more makeup than usual and seemed, to him, to be frenetic and far too talkative. He says he remembers having thought to himself, Kay looks manic. I, on the other hand, had thought I was splendid.

My mind was beginning to have to scramble a bit to keep up with itself, as ideas were coming so fast that they intersected one another at every conceivable angle. There was a neuronal pileup on the highways of my brain, and the more I tried to slow down my thinking the more I became aware that I couldn't. My enthusiasms were going into overdrive as well, although there often was some underlying thread of logic in what I was doing. One day, for example, I got into a frenzy of photocopying: I made thirty to forty copies of a poem by Edna St. Vincent Millay, an article about religion and psychosis from the *American Journal of Psychiatry,* and another article, "Why I Do Not Attend Case Conferences," written by a prominent psychologist who had elucidated all of the reasons why teaching rounds, when poorly conducted, are such a horrendous waste of time. All three of these articles seemed to me, quite suddenly, to have profound meaning and relevance for the clinical staff on the ward. So I passed them out to everyone I could.

What is interesting to me now is not that I did such a typically manic thing; rather, it's that there was some prescience and sense in those early days of incipient madness. The ward rounds *were* a complete waste of time, although the ward chief was less than appreciative of my pointing it out to everyone (and even less appreciative of my circulating the article to the entire staff). The Millay poem, "Renascence," was one I had read as a young girl, and, as my mood became more and more ecstatic, and my mind started racing ever and ever faster, I somehow remembered it with utter clarity and straightaway looked it up. Although I was just beginning my journey into madness, the poem described the entire cycle I was about to go through: it started with normal perceptions of the world ("All I could see from where I stood / Was three long mountains and a wood") and then continued through ecstatic and visionary states to unremitting despair and, finally, reemergence into the normal world, but with heightened awareness. Millay was nineteen years old when she wrote the poem, and, although I did not know it at the time, she later survived several breakdowns and hospitalizations. Somehow, in the strange state I was in, I knew that the poem had meaning for me; I understood it totally. I gave it to the residents and interns as a metaphorical description of the psychotic process and the important possibilities in a subsequent renewal. The residents, unaware of the internal flurry that propelled the readings, seemed to respond well to the articles and, almost to the person, expressed pleasure in the break from their regular medical reading.

During this same period of increasingly feverish behavior at work, my marriage was falling apart. I separated from my husband, ostensibly because I wanted children and he didn't—which was true and important—but it was far more complicated than that. I was increasingly restless, irritable, and I craved excitement; all of a sudden, I found myself rebelling against the very things I most loved about my husband: his kindness, stability, warmth, and love. I impulsively reached out for a new life. I found an exceedingly modern apartment in Santa Monica, although I hated modern architecture; I bought modern Finnish furniture, although I loved warm and old-fashioned things. Everything I acquired was cool, modern, angular, and, I suppose, strangely soothing and relatively uninvasive of my increasingly chaotic mind and jangled senses. There was, at least, a spectacular—and spectacularly expensive—view of the ocean. Spending a lot of money that you don't have—or, as the formal diagnostic criteria so quaintly put it, "engaging in unrestrained buying sprees"—is a classic part of mania.

When I am high I couldn't worry about money if I tried. So I don't. The money will come from somewhere; I am entitled; God will provide. Credit cards are disastrous, personal checks worse. Unfortunately, for manics anyway, mania is a natural extension of the economy. What with credit cards and bank accounts there is little beyond reach. So I bought twelve snakebite kits, with a sense of urgency and importance. I bought precious stones, elegant and unnecessary furniture, three watches within an hour of one another (in the Rolex rather than Timex class: champagne tastes bubble to the surface, are the surface, in mania), and totally inappropriate sirenlike clothes. During one spree in London I spent several hundred pounds on books having titles or covers that somehow caught my fancy: books on the natural history of the mole, twenty sundry Penguin books because I thought it could be nice if the penguins could form a colony. Once I think I shoplifted a blouse because I could not wait a minute longer for the woman-with-molasses feet in front of me in line. Or maybe I just thought about shoplifting, I don't remember, I was totally confused. I imagine I must have spent far more than thirty thousand dollars during my two major manic episodes, and God only knows how much more during my frequent milder manias.

But then back on lithium and rotating on the planet at the same pace as everyone else, you find your credit is decimated, your mortification complete: mania is not a luxury one can easily afford. It is devastating to have the illness and aggravating to have to pay for medications, blood tests, and psychotherapy. They, at least, are partially deductible. But money spent while manic doesn't fit into the Internal Revenue Service concept of medical expense or business loss. So after mania, when most depressed, you're given excellent reason to be even more so.

*H*aving a Ph.D. in economics from Harvard in no way prepared my brother for the sprawling financial mess he saw on the floor in front of him. There were piles of credit card receipts, stacks of pink overdraft notices from my bank, and duplicate and triplicate billings from all of the stores through which I had so recently swirled and charged. In a separate, more ominous pile were threatening letters from collection agencies. The chaotic visual impact upon entering the room reflected the higgledy-piggledy, pixilated collection of electric lobes that only a few weeks earlier had constituted my manic brain. Now, medicated and dreary, I was obsessively sifting through the remnants of my fiscal irresponsibility. It was like going on an archaeological dig through earlier ages of one's mind. There was a bill from a taxidermist in The Plains, Virginia, for example, for a stuffed fox that I for some reason had felt I desperately needed. I had loved animals all of my life, had at one point wanted to be a veterinarian: How on earth could I have bought a *dead* animal? I had adored foxes and admired them for as long as I could remember; I thought them fast and smart and beautiful: How could I have so directly contributed to killing one? I was appalled by the grisly nature of my purchase, disgusted with myself, and incapable of imagining what I would do with the fox once it actually arrived.

In an attempt to divert myself, I began pawing my way through the credit card slips. Near the top of the pile was a bill from the pharmacy where I had gotten my snakebite kits. The pharmacist, having just filled my first prescription for lithium, had smiled knowingly as he rang up the sale for my snakebite kits and the other absurd, useless, and bizarre purchases. I knew what he was thinking and, in the benevolence of my expansive mood, could appreciate the humor. He, unlike me, however, appeared to be completely unaware of the life-threatening problem created by rattlesnakes in the San Fernando Valley. God had chosen me, and apparently *only* me, to alert the world to the wild proliferation of killer snakes in the Promised Land. Or so I thought in my scattered delusional meanderings. In my own small way, by buying up the drugstore's entire supply of snakebite kits, I was doing all I could do to protect myself and those I cared about. In the midst of my crazed scurryings up and down the aisles of the drugstore, I had also come up with a plan to alert the *Los Angeles Times* to the danger. I was, however, far too manic to tie my thoughts together into a coherent plan.

My brother, seemingly having read my mind, walked into the room with a bottle of champagne and glasses on a tray. He imagined, he said, that we would need the champagne because the whole business might be a "bit unpleasant." My brother is not one for overstatement. Neither is he one for great wringings of hands and gnashings of teeth. He is, instead, a fair and practical man, generous, and one who, because of his own confidence, tends to inspire confidence in others. In all of these things, he is very much like our mother. During the time of my parents' separation, and subsequent divorce, he had put his wing out and around me, protecting me to the extent that he could from life's hurts and my own turbulent moods. His wing has been reliably available ever since. From the time I started college and then throughout my graduate and faculty days— indeed, until now, and still—whenever I have needed a respite from pain or uncertainty, or just to get away, I have found an airplane ticket in the mail, with a note suggesting I join him someplace like Boston or New York, or Colorado, or San Francisco. Often, he will be in one of these places to give a talk, consult, or take a few days off from work himself; I catch up with him in some hotel lobby or another, or in a posh restaurant, delighted to see him—tall, handsome, well dressed— walking quickly across the room. No matter my mood or problem, he always manages to make me feel that he is glad to see me. And each of the times I went abroad to live—first to Scotland as an undergraduate, then to England as a graduate student, and twice again to London on sabbatical leaves from the University of California—I always knew that it would be only a matter of weeks until he would arrive to check out where I was living, what I was up to, take me out to dinner, and suggest we rummage together through Hatchards or Dillons or some other bookstore. After my first severe manic attack, he drew his wing around me even tighter. He made it unequivocally clear that if I needed him, no matter where he was, he would be on the next plane home.

Now he made no judgments about my completely irrational purchases; or, if he did, at least he didn't make them to me. Courtesy of a personal loan he had taken out from the credit union at the World Bank, where he worked as an economist, we were able to write checks to cover all of the outstanding bills. Slowly, over a period of many years, I was able to pay him back what I owed him. More accurate, I was able to pay back the money I owed him. I can never pay back the love, kindness, and understanding.

I kept on with my life at a frightening pace. I worked ridiculously long hours and slept next to not at all. When I went home at night it was to a place of increasing chaos: Books, many of them newly purchased, were strewn everywhere. Clothes were piled up in mounds in every room, and there were unwrapped packages and unemptied shopping bags as far as the eye could see. My apartment looked like it had been inhabited and then abandoned by a colony of moles. There were hundreds of scraps of paper as well; they cluttered the top of my desk and kitchen counters, forming their own little mounds on the floor. One scrap contained an incoherent and rambling poem; I found it weeks later in my refrigerator, apparently triggered by my spice collection, which, needless to say, had grown by leaps and bounds during my mania. I had titled it, for reasons that I am sure made sense at the time, "God Is a Herbivore." There were many such poems and fragments, and they were everywhere. Weeks after I finally cleaned up my apartment, I still was coming across bits and pieces of paper—filled to the edges with writing—in unimaginably unlikely places.

My awareness and experience of sounds in general and music in particular were intense. Individual notes from a horn, an oboe, or a cello became exquisitely poignant. I heard each note alone, all notes together, and then each and all with piercing beauty and clarity. I felt as though I were standing in the orchestra pit; soon, the intensity and sadness of classical music became unbearable to me. I became impatient with the pace, as well as overwhelmed by the emotion. I switched abruptly to rock music, pulled out my Rolling Stones albums, and played them as loud as possible. I went from cut to cut, album to album, matching mood to music, music to mood. Soon my rooms were further strewn with records, tapes, and album jackets as I went on my way in search of the perfect sound. The chaos in my mind began to mirror the chaos of my rooms; I could no longer process what I was hearing; I became confused, scared, and disoriented. I could not listen for more than a few minutes to any particular piece of music; my behavior was frenetic, and my mind more so.

Slowly the darkness began to weave its way into my mind, and before long I was hopelessly out of control. I could not follow the path of my own thoughts. Sentences flew around in my head and fragmented first into phrases and then words; finally, only sounds remained. One evening I stood in the middle of my living room and looked out at a blood-red sunset spreading out over the horizon of the Pacific. Suddenly I felt a strange sense of light at the back of my eyes and almost immediately saw a huge black centrifuge inside my head. I saw a tall figure in a floor-length evening gown approach the centrifuge with a vase-sized glass tube of blood in her hand. As the figure turned around I saw to my horror that it was me and that there was blood all over my dress, cape, and long white gloves. I watched as the figure carefully put the tube of blood into one of the holes in the rack of the centrifuge, closed the lid, and pushed a button on the front of the machine. The centrifuge began to whirl.

Then, horrifyingly, the image that previously had been inside my head now was completely outside of it. I was paralyzed by fright. The spinning of the centrifuge and the clanking of the glass tube against the metal became louder and louder, and then the machine splintered into a thousand pieces. Blood was everywhere. It spattered against the windowpanes, against the walls and paintings, and soaked down into the carpets. I looked out toward the ocean and saw that the blood on the window had merged into the sunset; I couldn't tell where one ended and the other began. I screamed at the top of my lungs. I couldn't get away from the sight of the blood and the echoes of the machine's clanking as it whirled faster and faster. Not only had my thoughts spun wild, they had turned into an awful phantasmagoria, an apt but terrifying vision of an entire life and mind out of control. I screamed again and again. Slowly the hallucination receded. I telephoned a colleague for help, poured myself a large scotch, and waited for his arrival.

*F*ortunately, before my mania could become very public, this colleague—a man whom I had been dating during my separation from my husband, and someone who knew and understood me very well—was willing to take on my manic wrath and delusions. He confronted me with the need to take lithium, which was not a pleasant task for him—I was wildly agitated, paranoid, and physically violent—but it was one he carried out with skill, grace, and understanding. He was very gentle but insistent when he told me that he thought I had manic-depressive illness, and he persuaded me to make an appointment to see a psychiatrist. Together we tracked down everything we could find that had been written about the illness; we read as much as we could absorb and then moved on to what was known about treatment. Lithium had been approved for use in mania only four years earlier, in 1970, by the Food and Drug Administration, and was not yet in widespread use in California. It was clear from reading the medical literature, however, that lithium was the only drug that had any serious chance of working for me. He prescribed lithium and other antipsychotic medications for me, on a very short-term, emergency basis, only long enough to tide me over until I saw my psychiatrist for the first time. He put the correct number of pills out for me to take each morning and evening, and he spent hours talking with my family about my illness and how they might best handle it. He drew blood for several lithium levels and provided encouragement about the prognosis for my recovery. He also insisted that I take a short time off from work, which ultimately saved me from losing my job and my clinical privileges, and arranged for me to be looked after at home during those periods when he was unable to.

I felt infinitely worse, more dangerously depressed, during this first manic episode than when in the midst of my worst depressions. In fact, the most dreadful I had ever felt in my entire life—one characterized by chaotic ups and downs—was the first time I was psychotically manic. I had been mildly manic many times before, but these had never been frightening experiences—ecstatic at best, confusing at worst. I had learned to accommodate quite well to them. I had developed mechanisms of self-control, to keep down the peals of singularly inappropriate laughter, and set rigid limits on my irritability. I avoided situations that might otherwise trip or jangle my hypersensitive wiring, and I learned to pretend I was paying attention or following a logical point when my mind was off chasing rabbits in a thousand directions. My work and professional life flowed. But nowhere did this, or my upbringing, or my intellect, or my character, prepare me for insanity.

Although I had been building up to it for weeks, and certainly knew something was seriously wrong, there was a definite point when I knew I was insane. My thoughts were so fast that I couldn't remember the beginning of a sentence halfway through. Fragments of ideas, images, sentences, raced around and around in my mind like the tigers in a children's story. Finally, like those tigers, they became meaningless melted pools. Nothing once familiar to me was familiar. I wanted desperately to slow down but could not. Nothing helped—not running around a parking lot for hours on end or swimming for miles. My energy level was untouched by anything I did. Sex became too intense for pleasure, and during it I would feel my mind encased by black lines of light that were terrifying to me. My delusions centered on the slow painful deaths of all the green plants in the world—vine by vine, stem by stem, leaf by leaf they died, and I could do nothing to save them. Their screams were cacophonous. Increasingly, all of my images were black and decaying.

At one point I was determined that if my mind—by which I made my living and whose stability I had assumed for so many years—did not stop racing and begin working normally again, I would kill myself by jumping from a nearby twelve-story building. I gave it twenty-four hours. But, of course, I had no notion of time, and a million other thoughts—magnificent and morbid—wove in and raced by. Endless and terrifying days of endlessly terrifying drugs—Thorazine, lithium, valium, and barbiturates—finally took effect. I could feel my mind being reined in, slowed down, and put on hold. But it was a very long time until I recognized my mind again, and much longer until I trusted it.

I first met the man who was to become my psychiatrist when he was chief resident at the UCLA Neuropsychiatric Institute. Tall, good-looking, and a man of strong opinions, he had a steel-trap mind, a quick wit, and an easy laugh that softened an otherwise formidable presence. He was tough, disciplined, knew what he was doing, and cared very much about how he did it. He genuinely loved being a doctor, and he was a superb teacher. During my year as a predoctoral clinical psychology intern he had been assigned to supervise my clinical work on the adult inpatient service. He turned out to be an island of rational thought, rigorous diagnosis, and compassion in a ward situation where fragile egos and vapid speculation about intrapsychic and sexual conflicts prevailed. Although he was adamant about the importance of early and aggressive medical treatments for psychotic patients, he also had a genuine and deep belief in the importance of psychotherapy in bringing about healing and lasting change. His kindness to patients, combined with an extremely keen knowledge of medicine, psychiatry, and human nature, made a critical impression upon me. When I became violently manic just after joining the UCLA faculty, he was the only one I trusted with my mind and life. I knew intuitively that there wasn't a snowball's chance in hell that I could outtalk, outthink, or outmaneuver him. In the midst of utter confusion, it was a remarkably clear and sane decision.

I was not only very ill when I first called for an appointment, I was also terrified and deeply embarrassed. I had never been to a psychiatrist or a psychologist before. I had no choice. I had completely, but completely, lost my mind; if I didn't get professional help, I was quite likely to lose my job, my already precarious marriage, and my life as well. I drove from my office at UCLA to his office in the San Fernando Valley; it was an early southern California evening, usually a lovely time of day, but I was—for the first time in my life—shaking with fear. I shook for what he might tell me, and I shook for what he might not be able to tell me. For once, I could not begin to think or laugh my way out of the situation I was in, and I had no idea whether anything existed that would make me better.

I pushed the elevator button and walked down a long corridor to a waiting room. Two other patients were waiting for their doctors, which only added to my sense of indignity and embarrassment at finding myself with the roles reversed—character building, no doubt, but I was beginning to tire of all the opportunities to build character at the expense of peace, predictability, and a normal life. Perhaps, had I not been so vulnerable at the time, all of this would not have mattered so much. But I was confused and frightened and terribly shattered in all of my notions of myself; my self-confidence, which had permeated every aspect of my life for as long as I could remember, had taken a very long and disquieting holiday.

On the far wall of the waiting room I saw an array of lit and unlit buttons. It was clear I was supposed to push one of them; this, in turn, would let my psychiatrist-to-be know that I had arrived. I felt like a large white rat pressing paw to lever for a pellet. It was a strangely degrading, albeit practical, system. I had the sinking feeling that being on the wrong side of the desk was not going to sit very well with me.

My psychiatrist opened the door and, taking one long look at me, sat me down and said something reassuring. I have completely forgotten what it was—and I am sure it was as much the manner in which it was said as the actual words—but slowly a tiny, very tiny, bit of light drifted into my dark and frightened mind. I have next to no memory of what I said during that first session, but I know it was rambling, unstrung, and confused. He sat there, listening forever, it seemed, his long six-foot-four-inch frame spread out from chair to floor, legs tangling and untangling, long hands touching, fingertip to fingertip—and then he started asking questions.

How many hours of sleep had I been getting? Did I have any problems in concentrating? Had I been more talkative than usual? Did I talk faster than usual? Had anyone told me to slow down or that they couldn't make sense out of what I was saying? Had I felt a pressure to talk constantly? Had I been more energetic than usual? Were other people saying that they were having difficulty keeping up with me? Had I become more involved in activities than usual, or undertaken more projects? Had my thoughts been going so quickly that I had difficulty keeping track of them? Had I been more physically restless or agitated than usual? More sexually active? Had I been spending more money? Acting impulsively? Had I been more irritable or angry than usual? Had I felt as though I had special talents or powers? Had I had any visions or heard sounds or voices that other people probably hadn't seen or heard? Had I experienced any strange sensations in my body? Had I ever had any of these symptoms earlier in my life? Did anyone else in my family have similar sorts of problems?

I realized that I was on the receiving end of a very thorough psychiatric history and examination; the questions were familiar, I had asked them of others a hundred times, but I found it unnerving to have to answer them, unnerving not to know where it all was going, and unnerving to realize how confusing it was to be a patient. I answered yes to virtually all of his questions, including a long series of additional ones about depression, and found myself gaining a new respect for psychiatry and professionalism.

Gradually, his experience as a physician, and self-confidence as a person, began to take effect, much in the same way that medications gradually begin to take hold and calm the turmoil of mania. He made it unambivalently clear that he thought I had manic-depressive illness and that I was going to need to be on lithium, probably indefinitely. The thought was very frightening to me—much less was known then than is known now about the illness and its prognosis—but all the same I was relieved: relieved to hear a diagnosis that I knew in my mind of minds to be true. Still, I flailed against the sentence I felt he had handed me. He listened patiently. He listened to all of my convoluted, alternative explanations for my breakdown—the stress of a stressed marriage, the stress of joining the psychiatry faculty, the stress of overwork—and he remained firm in his diagnosis and recommendations for treatment. I was bitterly resentful, but somehow greatly relieved. And I respected him enormously for his clarity of thought, his obvious caring, and his unwillingness to equivocate in delivering bad news.

Over the next many years, except when I was living in England, I saw him at least once a week; when I was extremely depressed and suicidal I saw him more often. He kept me alive a thousand times over. He saw me through madness, despair, wonderful and terrible love affairs, disillusionments and triumphs, recurrences of illness, an almost fatal suicide attempt, the death of a man I greatly loved, and the enormous pleasures and aggravations of my professional life—in short, he saw me through the beginnings and endings of virtually every aspect of my psychological and emotional life. He was very tough, as well as very kind, and even though he understood more than anyone how much I felt I was losing—in energy, vivacity, and originality—by taking medication, he never was seduced into losing sight of the overall perspective of how costly, damaging, and life threatening my illness was. He was at ease with ambiguity, had a comfort with complexity, and was able to be decisive in the midst of chaos and uncertainty. He treated me with respect, a decisive professionalism, wit, and an unshakable belief in my ability to get well, compete, and make a difference.

Although I went to him to be treated for an illness, he taught me, by example, for my own patients, the total beholdenness of brain to mind and mind to brain. My temperament, moods, and illness clearly, and deeply, affected the relationships I had with others and the fabric of my work. But my moods were themselves powerfully shaped by the same relationships and work. The challenge was in learning to understand the complexity of this mutual beholdenness and in learning to distinguish the roles of lithium, will, and insight in getting well and leading a meaningful life. It was the task and gift of psychotherapy.

At this point in my existence, I cannot imagine leading a normal life without both taking lithium and having had the benefits of psychotherapy. Lithium prevents my seductive but disastrous highs, diminishes my depressions, clears out the wool and webbing from my disordered thinking, slows me down, gentles me out, keeps me from ruining my career and relationships, keeps me out of a hospital, alive, and makes psychotherapy possible.

But, ineffably, psychotherapy heals. *It makes some sense of the confusion, reins in the terrifying thoughts and feelings, returns some control and hope and possibility of learning from it all. Pills cannot, do not, ease one back into reality; they only bring one back headlong, careening, and faster than can be endured at times. Psychotherapy is a sanctuary; it is a battleground; it is a place I have been psychotic, neurotic, elated, confused, and despairing beyond belief. But, always, it is where I have believed—or have learned to believe—that I might someday be able to contend with all of this.*

No pill can help me deal with the problem of not wanting to take pills; likewise, no amount of psychotherapy alone can prevent my manias and depressions. I need both. It is an odd thing, owing life to pills, one's own quirks and tenacities, and this unique, strange, and ultimately profound relationship called psychotherapy.

*T*hat I owed my life to pills was not, however, obvious to me for a long time; my lack of judgment about the necessity to take lithium proved to be an exceedingly costly one.

Missing Saturn

*P*eople go mad in idiosyn-
cratic ways. Perhaps it was not surprising that, as a meteorologist's daughter, I found myself, in that glorious
illusion of high summer days, gliding, flying, now and
again lurching through cloud banks and ethers, past
stars, and across fields of ice crystals. Even now, I can see
in my mind's rather peculiar eye an extraordinary shattering and shifting of light; inconstant but ravishing colors laid out across miles of circling rings; and the almost
imperceptible, somehow surprisingly pallid, moons of
this Catherine wheel of a planet. I remember singing
"Fly Me to the Moons" as I swept past those of Saturn,
and thinking myself terribly funny. I saw and experienced that which had been only dreams, or fitful fragments of aspiration.

Was it real? Well, of course not, not in any meaningful sense of the word "real." But did it stay with me?
Absolutely. Long after my psychosis cleared, and the
medications took hold, it became part of what one
remembers forever, surrounded by an almost Proustian

melancholy. Long since that extended voyage of my mind and soul, Saturn and its icy rings took on an elegiac beauty, and I don't see Saturn's image now without feeling an acute sadness at its being so far away from me, so unobtainable in so many ways. The intensity, glory, and absolute assuredness of my mind's flight made it very difficult for me to believe, once I was better, that the illness was one I should willingly give up. Even though I was a clinician and a scientist, and even though I could read the research literature and see the inevitable, bleak consequences of not taking lithium, I for many years after my initial diagnosis was reluctant to take my medications as prescribed. Why was I so unwilling? Why did it take having to go through more episodes of mania, followed by long suicidal depressions, before I would take lithium in a medically sensible way?

Some of my reluctance, no doubt, stemmed from a fundamental denial that what I had was a real disease. This is a common reaction that follows, rather counterintuitively, in the wake of early episodes of manic-depressive illness. Moods are such an essential part of the substance of life, of one's notion of oneself, that even psychotic extremes in mood and behavior somehow can be seen as temporary, even understandable, reactions to what life has dealt. In my case, I had a horrible sense of loss for who I had been and where I had been. It was difficult to give up the high flights of mind and mood, even though the depressions that inevitably followed nearly cost me my life.

My family and friends expected that I would welcome being "normal," be appreciative of lithium, and take in stride having normal energy and sleep. But if you have had stars at your feet and the rings of planets through your hands, are used to sleeping only four or five hours a night and now sleep eight, are used to staying up all night for days and weeks in a row and now cannot, it is a very real adjustment to blend into a three-piece-suit schedule, which, while comfortable to many, is new, restrictive, seemingly less productive, and maddeningly less intoxicating. People say, when I complain of being less lively, less energetic, less high-spirited, "Well, now you're just like the rest of us," meaning, among other things, to be reassuring. But I compare myself with my former self, not with others. Not only that, I tend to compare my current self with the best I have been, which is when I have been mildly manic. When I am my present "normal" self, I am far removed from when I have been my liveliest, most productive, most intense, most outgoing and effervescent. In short, for myself, I am a hard act to follow.

And I miss Saturn very much.

My war with lithium began not long after I started taking it. I was first prescribed lithium in the fall of 1974; by the early spring of 1975, against medical advice, I had stopped taking it. Once my initial mania had cleared and I had recovered from the terrible depression that followed in its wake, an army of reasons had gathered in my mind to form a strong line of resistance to taking medication. Some of the reasons were psychological in nature. Others were related to the side effects that I experienced from the high blood levels of lithium that were required, at least initially, to keep my illness in check. (In 1974 the standard medical practice was to maintain patients at considerably higher blood levels of lithium than is now the case. I have been taking a lower dose of lithium for many years, and virtually all of the problems I experienced earlier in the course of my treatment have disappeared.) The side effects I had for the first ten years were very difficult to handle. In a small minority of patients, including myself, the therapeutic level of lithium, the level at which it works, is perilously close to the toxic level.

There was never any question that lithium worked very well for me—my form of manic-depressive illness is a textbook case of the clinical features related to good lithium response: I have grandiose and expansive manias, a strong family history of manic-depressive illness, and my manias precede my depressions, rather than the other way around—but the drug strongly affected my mental life. I found myself beholden to medication that also caused severe nausea and vomiting many times a month—I often slept on my bathroom floor with a pillow under my head and my warm, woolen St. Andrews gown tucked over me—when, because of changes in salt levels, diet, exercise, or hormones, my lithium level would get too high. I have been violently ill more places than I choose to remember, and quite embarrassingly so in public places ranging from lecture halls and restaurants to the National Gallery in London. (All of this changed very much for the better when I switched to a time-released preparation of lithium.) When I got particularly toxic I would start trembling, become ataxic and walk into walls, and my speech would become slurred; this resulted not only in several trips to the emergency room, where I would get intravenous drips to deal with the toxicity, but, much more mortifying, make me appear as though I were on illicit drugs or had had far too much to drink.

One evening, after a riding lesson in Malibu during which I twice fell off my horse into the poles of a jump, I was pulled over to the side of the road by the police. They put me through an impressively thorough roadside neurological exam—I walked a not very straight line; was not able to make my fingertip reach my nose; and was hopelessly bad at getting my fingertips to tap against my thumb; God only knows what the pupils of my eyes were doing when a police officer blared a light into them—and until I got out my bottles of medication, gave the officers the name and telephone number of my psychiatrist, and agreed to whatever blood tests they wanted to order, the police refused to believe that I was not on drugs or hadn't been drinking.

Not long after that incident, shortly after I learned to ski, I was on a very tall mountain somewhere in Utah and unaware that high altitude coupled with rigorous exercise can raise lithium levels. I became completely disoriented and totally incapable of navigating my way down the mountain. Fortunately, a colleague of mine who knew I was taking lithium, and who was himself an expert on its medical uses, became concerned when I didn't catch up with him at the time we had arranged to meet. He concluded that I might have become toxic from it, sent the ski patrol after me, and I came down the mountain safely, although rather more horizontally than I would have liked.

Nausea and vomiting and occasional toxicity, while upsetting and embarrassing at times, were far less important to me than lithium's effect on my ability to read, comprehend, and remember what I read. In rare

instances, lithium causes problems of visual accommo-
dation, which can, in turn, lead to a form of blurred
vision. It also can impair concentration and attention
span and affect memory. Reading, which had been at
the heart of my intellectual and emotional existence,
was suddenly beyond my grasp. I was used to reading
three or four books a week; now it was impossible. I did
not read a serious work of literature or nonfiction,
cover to cover, for more than ten years. The frustration
and pain of this were immeasurable. I threw books
against the wall in a blind fury and sailed medical journals across my office in a rage. I could read journal articles better than books, because they were short; but it
was with great difficulty, and I had to read the same
lines repeatedly and take copious notes before I could
comprehend the meaning. Even so, what I read often
disappeared from my mind like snow on a hot pave-
ment. I took up needlepoint as a diversion and made
countless cushions and firescreens in a futile attempt to
fill the hours I had previously filled with reading.

Poetry, thank God, remained within my grasp, and,
having always loved it, I now fell upon it with a passion
that is hard to describe. I found that children's books,
which, in addition to being shorter than books written
for adults, also had larger print, were relatively accessible to me, and I read over and over again the classics of
childhood—*Peter Pan, Mary Poppins, Charlotte's Web,
Huckleberry Finn,* the Oz books, *Doctor Dolittle*—that
had once, so many years earlier, opened up such unforgettable worlds to me. Now they gave me a second
chance, a second wind of pleasure and beauty. But of all
the children's books, I returned most often to *The Wind
in the Willows.* I found myself occasionally totally over-

whelmed by it. Once, I remember, I broke down entirely at a particular passage describing Mole and his house. I cried and cried and could not stop.

Recently, I pulled down my copy of *The Wind in the Willows*, which had remained on the bookshelf unopened once I had regained my ability to read, and tried to track down what it was that had created such a shattering reaction. After a brief search I found the passage I had been looking for. Mole, who had been away from his underground home for a very long time exploring the world of light and adventure with his friend Ratty, one winter evening is walking along and suddenly and powerfully, with "recollection in fullest flood," smells his old home. Desperate to revisit it, he struggles to persuade the Rat to accompany him:

> *"Please stop, Ratty!" pleaded the poor Mole, in anguish of heart. "You don't understand! It's my home, my old home! I've just come across the smell of it, and it's close by here, really quite close. And I must go to it, I must, I must! O, come back, Ratty! Please, please come back!"*

The Rat, initially preoccupied and reluctant to take the time to do so, finally does visit Mole in his home. Later, after Christmas carols and a nightcap of mulled ale in front of the fire, Mole reflects on how much he has missed the warmth and security of what he once had known, all of those "friendly things which had long been unconsciously a part of him." At this point in my rereading, I remembered exactly, and with visceral force, what I had felt reading it not long after I had started taking lithium: I missed my home, my mind, my life of books and "friendly things," my world where most things were in their place, and where nothing awful could come in to wreck havoc. Now I had no choice but to live in the broken world that my mind had forced upon me. I longed for the days that I had known before madness and medication had insinuated their way into every aspect of my existence.

Rules for the Gracious Acceptance of Lithium
into Your Life

1. *Clear out the medicine cabinet before guests arrive for dinner or new lovers stay the night.*
2. *Remember to put the lithium back into the cabinet the next day.*
3. *Don't be too embarrassed by your lack of coordination or your inability to do well the sports you once did with ease.*
4. *Learn to laugh about spilling coffee, having the palsied signature of an eighty-year-old, and being unable to put on cuff links in less than ten minutes.*
5. *Smile when people joke about how they think they "need to be on lithium."*
6. *Nod intelligently, and with conviction, when your physician explains to you the many advantages of lithium in leveling out the chaos in your life.*
7. *Be patient when waiting for this leveling off. Very patient. Reread the Book of Job. Continue being patient. Contemplate the similarity between the phrases "being patient" and "being a patient."*

8. *Try not to let the fact that you can't read without effort annoy you. Be philosophical. Even if you could read, you probably wouldn't remember most of it anyway.*

9. *Accommodate to a certain lack of enthusiasm and bounce that you once had. Try not to think about all the wild nights you once had. Probably best not to have had those nights anyway.*

10. *Always keep in perspective how much better you are. Everyone else certainly points it out often enough, and, annoyingly enough, it's probably true.*

11. *Be appreciative. Don't even consider stopping your lithium.*

12. *When you do stop, get manic, get depressed, expect to hear two basic themes from your family, friends, and healers:*
    - *But you were doing so much better, I just don't understand it.*
    - *I told you this would happen.*

13. *Restock your medicine cabinet.*

*P*sychological issues ultimately proved far more important than side effects in my prolonged resistance to lithium. I simply did not want to believe that I needed to take medication. I had become addicted to my high moods; I had become dependent upon their intensity, euphoria, assuredness, and their infectious ability to induce high moods and enthusiasms in other people. Like gamblers who sacrifice everything for the fleeting but ecstatic moments of winning, or cocaine addicts who risk their families, careers, and lives for brief interludes of high energy and mood, I found my milder manic states powerfully inebriating and very conducive to productivity. I couldn't give them up. More fundamentally, I genuinely believed—courtesy of strong-willed parents, my own stubbornness, and a WASP military upbringing—that I ought to be able to handle whatever difficulties came my way without having to rely upon crutches such as medication.

I was not the only one who felt this way. When I became ill, my sister was adamant that I should not take lithium and was disgusted that I did. In an odd reversion to the Puritan upbringing she had raged against, she made it clear that she thought I should "weather it through" my depressions and manias, and that my soul would wither if I chose to dampen the intensity and pain of my experiences by using medication. The combination of her worsening moods with mine, along with the dangerous seductiveness of her views about medication, made it very difficult for me to maintain a relationship with her. One evening, now many years ago, she tore into me for "capitulating to Organized Medicine" by "lithiumizing away my feelings." My personality, she said, had dried up, the fire was going out, and I was but a shell of my former self. This hit an utterly raw nerve in me, as I imagine she knew it would, but it simply enraged the man I was going out with at the time. He had seen me very ill indeed and saw nothing of value to preserve in such insanity. He tried to deflect the situation with wit—"Your sister may be just a shell of her former self," he said, "but her shell is as much or more than I can handle"—but my sister then took off after him, leaving me sick inside, and doubtful, yet again, about my decision to take lithium.

I could not afford to be too near someone representing, as she did, the temptations residing in my unmedicated mind; the voice of upbringing that said one should be able to handle everything by oneself; the catnip allure of recapturing lost moods and ecstasies. I was beginning, but *just* beginning, to understand that not only my mind but also my life was at stake. I had not been brought up to submit without a fight, however. I really believed all of the things I had been taught about weathering it through, self-reliance, and not imposing your problems on other people. But looking back over the wreckage brought about by this kind of blind stupidity and pride, I now wonder, What on earth could I have been thinking? I also had been taught to think for myself: Why, then, didn't I question these rigid, irrelevant notions of self-reliance? Why didn't I see how absurd my defiance really was?

A few months ago I asked my psychiatrist for a copy of my medical records. When I read over them, it was a very disconcerting experience. By March of 1975, six months after starting lithium, I had stopped taking it. Within weeks I became manic and then severely depressed. Later that year I resumed my lithium. As I read through my doctor's notes for the time, I was appalled to find a continuation of the pattern:

7-17-75 *Patient has elected to resume lithium because of the severity of her depressive episodes. Will begin with lithium 300mg. BID [twice a day].*

7-25-75 *Vomiting.*

8-5-75   *Tolerating lithium. Feeling depressed at realization she was more hypomanic than she believed.*

9-30-75   *Patient has stopped lithium again. Very important, she says, to prove she can handle stress without it.*

10-2-75   *Persists in not taking lithium. Already hypomanic. Patient well aware of it.*

10-7-75   *Patient has resumed lithium because of increased irritability, insomnia, and inability to concentrate.*

Part of my stubbornness can be put down to human nature. It is hard for anyone with an illness, chronic or acute, to take medications absolutely as prescribed. Once the symptoms of an illness improve or go away, it becomes even more difficult. In my case, once I felt well again I had neither the desire nor incentive to continue taking my medication. I didn't want to take it to begin with; the side effects were hard for me to adjust to; I missed my highs; and, once I felt normal again, it was very easy for me to deny that I had an illness that would come back. Somehow I was convinced that I was an exception to the extensive research literature, which clearly showed not only that manic-depressive illness comes back, but that it often comes back in a more severe and frequent form.

It was not that I ever thought lithium was an ineffective drug. Far from it. The evidence for its efficacy and safety was compelling. Not only that, I knew it worked for me. It certainly was not that I had any moral arguments against psychiatric medications. On the contrary. I had, and have, no tolerance for those individuals—especially psychiatrists and psychologists—who oppose using medications for psychiatric illnesses; those clinicians who somehow draw a distinction between the suffering and treatability of "medical illnesses" such as Hodgkin's disease or breast cancer, and psychiatric illnesses such as depression, manic-depression, or schizophrenia. I believe, without doubt, that manic-depressive illness is a medical illness; I also believe that, with rare exception, it is malpractice to treat it without medication. All of these beliefs aside, however, I still somehow thought that I ought to be able to carry on without drugs, that I ought to be able to continue to do things my own way.

My psychiatrist, who took all of these complaints very seriously—existential qualms, side effects, matters of value from my upbringing—never wavered in his conviction that I needed to take lithium. He refused, thank God, to get drawn into my convoluted and impassioned web of reasoning about why I should try, just one more time, to survive without taking medication. He always kept the basic choice in perspective: The issue was not whether lithium was a problematic drug; it was not whether I missed my highs; it was not whether taking medication was consistent with some idealized notion of my family background. The underlying issue was whether or not I would choose to use lithium only intermittently, and thereby ensure a return of my manias and depressions. The choice, as he saw it—and as is now painfully clear to me—was between madness and sanity, and between life and death. My manias were occurring more frequently and, increasingly, were becoming more "mixed" in nature (that is, my predominantly euphoric episodes, those I thought of as my "white manias," were becoming more and more overlaid with agitated depressions); my depressions were getting worse and far more suicidal. Few medical treatments, as he pointed out, are free of side effects, and, all things considered, lithium causes fewer adverse reactions than most. Certainly, it was a vast improvement on the brutal and ineffectual treatments that preceded it—chains, bloodletting, wet packs, asylums, and ice picks through the lobes—and although the anticonvulsant medications now work very effectively, and often with fewer side effects, for many people who have manic-depressive illness, lithium remains an extremely effective drug. I knew all of this, although it was with less conviction than I have now.

In fact, underneath it all, I was actually secretly terrified that lithium might *not* work: What if I took it, and I still got sick? If, on the other hand, I didn't take it, I wouldn't have to see my worst fears realized. My psychiatrist very early on saw this terror in my soul, and there is one brief observation in his medical notes that captured this paralyzing fear completely: *Patient sees medication as a promise of a cure, and a means of suicide if it doesn't work. She fears that by taking it she will risk her last resort.*

*Y*ears later, I was in a hotel ballroom packed with more than a thousand psychiatrists, many of them in a feeding frenzy; free food and drinks, however abysmal, have a way of bringing doctors out of the woodwork and up to the troughs. Journalists and other writers often discuss the August migration of psychiatrists, but there is a different kind of herding behavior in May—the peak month for suicide, one might note—when fifteen thousand shrinks of all stripes attend the annual meeting of the American Psychiatric Association. Several of my colleagues and I were to give talks about recent advances in the diagnosis, pathophysiology, and treatment of manic-depressive illness. I was, of course, pleased that the disease I suffered from drew such a large crowd; it was in one of its vogue years, but I also knew that it was inevitable, in other years, that this role would be captured, in turn, by obsessive-compulsive disorder or multiple-personality disorder or panic disorder, or whatever other illness caught the fancy of the field, promised a new breakthrough treatment, had the most colorful PET (positron emission tomography) scan images, had been central to a particularly nasty and expensive lawsuit, or was becoming more readily reimbursable by insurance companies.

I was scheduled to speak about psychological and medical aspects of lithium treatment, so, as was often the case, I started off with a quote from "a patient with manic-depressive illness." I read it as if it had been written by someone else, although it was my own experience being recounted.

> The endless questioning finally ended. My psychiatrist looked at me, there was no uncertainty in his voice. "Manic-depressive illness." I admired his bluntness. I wished him locusts on his lands and a pox upon his house. Silent, unbelievable rage. I smiled pleasantly. He smiled back. The war had just begun.

The truth of the clinical situation hit a responsive chord, for it is an unusual psychiatrist who has not had to deal with the subtle, and not so subtle, resistance to treatment shown by many patients with manic-depressive illness. The final sentence, "The war had just begun," brought a roar of laughter. The humor, however, was a bit more in the recounting than in the actual living through it. Unfortunately, this resistance to taking lithium is played out in the lives of tens of thousands of patients every year. Almost always it leads to a recurrence of the illness; not uncommonly it results in tragedy. I was to see this, a few years after my own struggles with lithium, in a patient of mine. He became a particularly painful reminder to me of the high costs of defiance.

*T*he UCLA emergency room was alive with residents, interns, and medical students; it was also, rather strangely, very much alive with illness and death. People were moving quickly, with the kind of brisk self-assurance that high intelligence, good training, and demanding circumstances tend to breed; and, despite the unfortunate reason for my having been called down to the ER—one of my patients had been admitted acutely psychotic—I found myself unavoidably caught up in the exhilarating pace and chaotic rhythm. Then came an absolutely blood-curdling scream from one of the examining rooms—a scream of terror and undeniable madness—and I ran down the corridor: past the nurses, past a medical resident dictating notes for a patient's chart, and past a surgical resident poring over the *PDR* with a cup of coffee in one hand, a hemostat clamped and dangling from the short sleeve of his green scrub suit, and a stethoscope draped around his neck.

I opened the door to the room where the screams had begun, and my heart sank. The first person I saw was the psychiatry resident on call, whom I knew; he smiled sympathetically. Then I saw my patient, strapped down on a gurney, in four-point leather restraints. He was lying spread-eagle on his back, each wrist and ankle bound in a leather cuff, with an additional leather restraining strap across his chest. I felt sick to my stomach. Despite the restraints, I also felt scared. A year before this same patient had held a knife to my throat during a psychotherapy session in my office. I had called the police at that time, and he had been involuntarily committed to one of the locked wards at UCLA's Neuropsychiatric Institute. Seventy-two hours later, in the impressively blind wisdom of the American justice system, he had been released back into the community. And to my care. I noted with some irony that the three police officers who were standing by the gurney, two of whom had their hands resting on their guns, evidently thought he represented a "threat to himself or others" even if the judge hadn't.

He screamed again. It was a truly primitive and frightening sound, in part because he himself was so frightened, and in part because he was very tall, very big, and completely psychotic. I put my hand on his shoulder and could feel his whole body shaking out of control. I had never seen such fear in anyone's eyes, nor such visceral agitation and psychological pain. Delirious mania is many things, and all of them are awful beyond description. The resident had given him a massive injection of an antipsychotic medication, but the drug had not yet taken hold. He was delusional, paranoid, largely incoherent, and experiencing both visual and auditory hallucinations. He reminded me of films I had seen of horses trapped in fires with their eyes wild with fear and their bodies paralyzed in terror. I tightened my hand on his shoulder, shook him gently, and said, "It's Dr. Jamison. You've been given some Haldol; we're going to take you up to the ward. You're going to be all right." I caught his eye for a moment. Then he screamed again. "You'll be fine. I know you don't believe it now, but you will be well again." I looked over at the three thick volumes of his medical records lying on the table nearby, thought about his countless hospitalizations, and wondered about the truthfulness of my remarks.

That he would get well again, I had no doubt. How long it would last was another question. Lithium worked remarkably well for him, but once his hallucinations and abject terror stopped, he would quit taking it. Neither the resident nor I needed to see the results of the lithium blood level that had been drawn on his admission to the emergency room. There would be no lithium in his blood. The result had been mania. Suicidal depression would inevitably follow, as would the indescribable pain and disruptiveness to his life and to the lives of the members of his family. The severity of his depressions was a black mirror image of the dangerousness of his manias. In short, he had a particularly bad, although not uncommon, form of the illness; lithium worked well, but he wouldn't take it. In many ways, it seemed to me, as I stood there next to him in the emergency room, that all of the time, effort, and emotional energy that I and the others put into treating him were to little or no avail.

Gradually the Haldol began to take effect. The screaming stopped, and the frantic straining against his restraints died down. He was both less frightened and less frightening; after a while he said to me, in a slowed and slurred voice, "Don't leave me, Dr. Jamison. Please, please don't leave me." I assured him I would stay with him until he got to the ward. I knew that I was the one constant throughout all of his hospitalizations, court appearances, family meetings, and black depressions. As his psychotherapist for years, I had been privy to his dreams and fears, hopeful and then ruined relationships, grandiose and then shattered plans for the future. I had seen his remarkable resilience, personal courage, and wit; I liked and respected him enormously. But I also had been increasingly frustrated by his repeated refusals to take medication. I could, from my own experience, understand his concerns about taking lithium, but only up to a point; past that point, I was finding it very difficult to watch him go through such predictable, painful, and unnecessary recurrences of his illness.

No amount of psychotherapy, education, persuasion, or coercion worked; no contracts worked out by the medical and nursing staff worked; family therapy didn't help; no tallying up of the hospitalizations, broken relationships, financial disasters, lost jobs, imprisonments, squanderings of a good, creative, and educated mind worked. Nothing I or anyone else could think of worked. Over the years, I asked several of my colleagues to see him in consultation, but they, like me, could find no way to reach him, no chink in the tightly riveted armor of his resistance. I spent hours talking to my own psychiatrist about him, in part to seek his clinical advice, and in part to make sure that my own history of stopping and starting lithium was not playing some sort of unconscious, unacknowledged role. His attacks of mania and depression became more frequent and severe. No breakthrough ever came; no happy ending ever materialized. There was simply nothing that medicine or psychology could bring to bear that would make him take his medication long enough to stay well. Lithium worked, but he would not take it; our relationship worked, but not well enough. He had a terrible disease and it eventually cost him his life—as it does tens of thousands of people every year. There were limits on what any of us could do for him, and it tore me apart inside.

We all move uneasily within our restraints.

The Charnel House

I reaped a bitter harvest from
my own refusal to take lithium on a consistent basis. A
floridly psychotic mania was followed, inevitably, by a
long and lacerating, black, suicidal depression; it lasted
more than a year and a half. From the time I woke up in
the morning until the time I went to bed at night, I
was unbearably miserable and seemingly incapable of any
kind of joy or enthusiasm. Everything—every thought,
word, movement—was an effort. Everything that once
was sparkling now was flat. I seemed to myself to be dull,
boring, inadequate, thick brained, unlit, unresponsive,
chill skinned, bloodless, and sparrow drab. I doubted,
completely, my ability to do anything well. It seemed as
though my mind had slowed down and burned out to
the point of being virtually useless. The wretched, convoluted, and pathetically confused mass of gray worked
only well enough to torment me with a dreary litany of
my inadequacies and shortcomings in character, and to
taunt me with the total, the desperate, hopelessness of it
all. What is the point in going on like this? I would ask

myself. Others would say to me, "It is only temporary, it will pass, you will get over it," but of course they had no idea how I felt, although they were certain that they did. Over and over and over I would say to myself, If I can't feel, if I can't move, if I can't think, and I can't care, then what conceivable point is there in living?

The morbidity of my mind was astonishing: Death and its kin were constant companions. I saw Death everywhere, and I saw winding sheets and toe tags and body bags in my mind's eye. Everything was a reminder that everything ended at the charnel house. My memory always took the black line of the mind's underground system; thoughts would go from one tormented moment of my past to the next. Each stop along the way was worse than the preceding one. And, always, everything was an effort. Washing my hair took hours to do, and it drained me for hours afterward; filling the ice-cube tray was beyond my capacity, and I occasionally slept in the same clothes I had worn during the day because I was too exhausted to undress.

During this time I was seeing my psychiatrist two or three times a week and, finally, again taking lithium on a regular basis. His notes, in addition to keeping track of the medications I was taking—I had briefly taken antidepressants, for example, but they had only made me more dangerously agitated—also recorded the unrelenting, day-in and day-out, week-in and week-out, despair, hopelessness, and shame that the depression was causing: *"Patient intermittently suicidal. Wishes to jump from the top of hospital stairwell"; "Patient continues to be a significant suicide risk. Hospitalization is totally unacceptable to her and in my view she cannot be held under LPS [the California commitment law]"; "Despairs for the future; fears recurrence and fears having to deal with the fact that she has felt what she has felt"; "Patient feels very embarrassed about feelings she has and takes attitude that regardless of the course of her depression she 'won't put up with it' "; "Patient reluctant to be with people when depressed because she feels her depression is such an intolerable burden on others"; "Afraid to leave my office. Hasn't slept in days. Desperate."* At this point there was a brief lull in my depression, only to be followed by its seemingly inevitable, dreadful return: *"Patient feels as if she has cracked. Hopeless that depressed feelings have returned."*

My psychiatrist repeatedly tried to persuade me to go into a psychiatric hospital, but I refused. I was horrified at the thought of being locked up; being away from familiar surroundings; having to attend group therapy meetings; and having to put up with all of the indignities and invasions of privacy that go into being on a psychiatric ward. I was working on a locked ward at the time, and I didn't relish the idea of not having the key. Mostly, however, I was concerned that if it became public knowledge that I had been hospitalized, my clinical work and privileges at best would be suspended; at worst, they would be revoked on a permanent basis. I continued to resist voluntary hospitalization; and, because the California commitment code is designed more for the well-being of lawyers than of patients, it would have been relatively easy for me to talk my way out of an involuntary commitment. Even had I been committed, there was no guarantee at all that I would not have attempted or committed suicide while on the ward; psychiatric hospitals are not uncommon places for suicide. (After this experience, I drew up a clear arrangement with my psychiatrist and family that if I again become severely depressed they have the authority to approve, against my will if necessary, both electroconvulsive therapy, or ECT, an excellent treatment for certain types of severe depression, and hospitalization.)

At the time, nothing seemed to be working, despite excellent medical care, and I simply wanted to die and be done with it. I resolved to kill myself. I was cold-bloodedly determined not to give any indication of my plans or the state of my mind; I was successful. The only note made by my psychiatrist on the day before I attempted suicide was: *Severely depressed. Very quiet.*

In a rage I pulled the bathroom lamp off the wall and felt the violence go through me but not yet out of me. "For Christ's sake," he said, rushing in—and then stopping very quietly. Jesus, I must be crazy, I can see it in his eyes: a dreadful mix of concern, terror, irritation, resignation, and why me, Lord? "Are you hurt?" he asks. Turning my head with its fast-scanning eyes I see in the mirror blood running down my arms, collecting into the tight ribbing of my beautiful, erotic negligee, only an hour ago used in passion of an altogether different and wonderful kind. "I can't help it. I can't help it," I chant to myself, but I can't say it; the words won't come out, and the thoughts are going by far too fast. I bang my head over and over against the door. God make it stop, I can't stand it, I know I'm insane again. He really cares, I think, but within ten minutes he too is screaming, and his eyes have a wild look from contagious madness, from the lightning adrenaline between the two of us. "I can't leave you like this," but I say a few truly awful things and then go for his throat in a more literal way, and he does leave me, provoked beyond endurance and unable to see the devastation and despair inside. I can't convey it and he can't see it; there's nothing to be done. I can't think, I can't calm this murderous cauldron, my grand ideas of an hour ago seem absurd and pathetic, my life is in ruins and—worse still— ruinous; my body is uninhabitable. It is raging and weeping and full of destruction and wild energy gone amok. In the mirror I see a creature I don't know but must live and share my mind with.

I understand why Jekyll killed himself before Hyde had taken over completely. I took a massive overdose of lithium with no regrets.

Within psychiatric circles, if you kill yourself, you earn the right to be considered a "successful" suicide. This is a success one can live without. Suicidal depression, I decided in the midst of my indescribably awful, eighteen-month bout of it, is God's way of keeping manics in their place. It works. Profound melancholia is a day-in, day-out, night-in, night-out, almost arterial level of agony. It is a pitiless, unrelenting pain that affords no window of hope, no alternative to a grim and brackish existence, and no respite from the cold undercurrents of thought and feeling that dominate the horribly restless nights of despair. There is an assumption, in attaching Puritan concepts such as "successful" and "unsuccessful" to the awful, final act of suicide, that those who "fail" at killing themselves not only are weak, but incompetent, incapable even of getting their dying quite right. Suicide, however, is almost always an irrational act and seldom is it accompanied by the kind of rigorous intellect that goes with one's better days. It is also often impulsive and not necessarily undertaken in the way one originally planned.

I, for example, thought I had covered every contingency. I could not stand the pain any longer, could not abide the bone-weary and tiresome person I had become, and felt that I could not continue to be responsible for the turmoil I was inflicting upon my friends and family. In a perverse linking within my mind I thought that, like the pilot whom I had seen kill himself to save the lives of others, I was doing the only fair thing for the people I cared about; it was also the only sensible thing to do for myself. One would put an animal to death for far less suffering.

At one point I bought a gun, but, in a transient wave of rational thought, I told my psychiatrist; reluctantly, I got rid of it. Then for many months I went to the eighth floor of the stairwell of the UCLA hospital and, repeatedly, only just resisted throwing myself off the ledge. Suicidal depression does not tend to be a considerate, outward, or other-considering sort of state, but somehow the thought that my family would have to identify the fallen and fractured me made that ultimately not an acceptable method. So I decided upon a solution that seemed to me to be poetic in its full-circledness. Lithium, although it ultimately saved my life, at that particular time was causing me no end of grief and sorrow. So I decided to take a massive overdose.

In order to keep the lithium from being vomited back up, I had gone to an emergency room and obtained a prescription for an anti-emetic medication. I then waited for a break in the informal "suicide watch" that my friends and family, in conjunction with my psychiatrist, had put into place. This done, I removed the telephone from my bedroom so I would not inadvertently pick it up—I could not take the phone off its hook entirely as I knew this would alert my keepers—and, after a terrible row, and in a very agitated and violent state, I took handful after handful of pills. I then curled up in my bed and waited to die. I hadn't planned on the fact that one's drugged brain acts differently from one's alert brain. When the telephone rang I must have instinctively thought to answer it; thus I crawled, semi-comatose, to the telephone in the living room. My slurred voice alerted my brother, who was calling from Paris to see how I was doing. He immediately called my psychiatrist.

It was not a pleasant way not to commit suicide. Lithium is used to teach coyotes to stop killing sheep: often a single experience with a lithium-treated sheep carcass will make a coyote sick enough to keep his teeth to himself. Although I had taken medication to keep me from vomiting up the lithium, I still ended up sicker than a coyote, sicker than a dog, sicker than I could ever wish anyone to be. I also was in and out of a coma for several days, which, given the circumstances, was probably just as well.

For a long time both before and after I tried to kill myself, I was in the close care of a friend of mine, one who redefined for me the notion of friendship. He was a psychiatrist, as well as a warm, whimsical, and witty man who had a mind like a cluttered attic. He was intrigued by a variety of bizarre things, including me, and wrote fascinating articles about such topics as nutmeg psychoses and the personal habits of Sherlock Holmes. He was intensely loyal and spent evening after evening with me, somehow enduring my choleric moods. He was generous with both his time and money, and he stubbornly believed that I would make it through my depression and, ultimately, thrive.

Sometimes, after I had told him that I simply had to be alone, he would call me later, at one or two o'clock in the morning, to see how I was doing. He could tell from my voice what state I was in, and, despite my pleas to be left alone, he would insist on coming over. Often this was in the guise of "I can't sleep. You wouldn't refuse to keep a friend company, would you?" Knowing full well that he was only checking up on me, I would say, "Yes. Trust me. I can refuse. Leave me alone. I'm in a foul mood." He would call back again in a few minutes and say, "Please, please, pretty please. I really need the company. We can go somewhere and get some ice cream." So we would get together at some ungodly hour, I would be secretly and inexpressibly grateful, and he somehow would have finessed it so that I didn't feel like I was too huge a burden to him. It was a rare gift of friendship.

Fortuitously, he also worked as an emergency room physician on weekends. After my suicide attempt, he and my psychiatrist worked out a plan for my medical care and supervision. My friend kept a constant watch on me, drew my blood for lithium and electrolyte levels, and walked me repeatedly to pull me out of my drugged state, as one would move a sick shark around its tank in order to keep the water circulating through its gills. He was the only person I knew who could make me laugh during my truly morbid moments. Like my husband, from whom I was legally separated but still frequently in contact, he had a gentling and calming effect on me when I was vastly irritable, perturbed, or perturbing. He nursed me through the most awful days of my life, and it is to him, only next to my psychiatrist and family, that I most owe my life.

The debt I owe my psychiatrist is beyond description. I remember sitting in his office a hundred times during those grim months and each time thinking, What on earth can he say that will make me feel better or keep me alive? Well, there never was anything he could say, that's the funny thing. It was all the stupid, desperately optimistic, condescending things he *didn't* say that kept me alive; all the compassion and warmth I felt from him that could not have been said; all the intelligence, competence, and time he put into it; and his granite belief that mine was a life worth living. He was terribly direct, which was terribly important, and he was willing to admit the limits of his understanding and treatments and when he was wrong. Most difficult to put into words, but in many ways the essence of everything: He taught me that the road from suicide to life is cold and colder and colder still, but—with steely effort, the grace of God, and an inevitable break in the weather—that I could make it.

My mother also was wonderful. She cooked meal after meal for me during my long bouts of depression, helped me with my laundry, and helped pay my medical bills. She endured my irritability and boringly bleak moods, drove me to the doctor, took me to pharmacies, and took me shopping. Like a gentle mother cat who picks up a straying kitten by the nape of its neck, she kept her marvelously maternal eyes wide-open, and, if I floundered too far away, she brought me back into a geographic and emotional range of security, food, and protection. Her formidable strength slowly eked its way into my depleted marrowbone. It, coupled with medicine for my brain and superb psychotherapy for my mind, pulled me through day after impossibly hard day. Without her I never could have survived. There were times when I would struggle to put together a lecture, and, having no idea whether it made sense or not, I would deliver it through the din and dreadful confusion that masqueraded as my mind. Often the only thing that would keep me going was the belief, instilled by my mother years before, that will and grit and responsibility are what ultimately make us supremely human in our existence. For each terrible storm that came my way, my mother—her love and her strong sense of values—provided me with powerful, and sustaining, countervailing winds.

The complexities of what we are given in life are vast and beyond comprehension. It was as if my father had given me, by way of temperament, an impossibly wild, dark, and unbroken horse. It was a horse without a name, and a horse with no experience of a bit between its teeth. My mother taught me to gentle it; gave me the discipline and love to break it; and—as Alexander had known so intuitively with Bucephalus—she understood, and taught me, that the beast was best handled by turning it toward the sun.

*B*oth my manias and depressions had violent sides to them. Violence, especially if you are a woman, is not something spoken about with ease. Being wildly out of control—physically assaultive, screaming insanely at the top of one's lungs, running frenetically with no purpose or limit, or impulsively trying to leap from cars—is frightening to others and unspeakably terrifying to oneself. In blind manic rages I have done all of these things, at one time or another, and some of them repeatedly; I remain acutely and painfully aware of how difficult it is to control or understand such behaviors, much less explain them to others. I have, in my psychotic, seizurelike attacks—my black, agitated manias—destroyed things I cherish, pushed to the utter edge people I love, and survived to think I could never recover from the shame. I have been physically restrained by terrible, brute force; kicked and pushed to the floor; thrown on my stomach with my hands pinned behind my back; and heavily medicated against my will.

I do not know how I have recovered from having done the things that necessitated such actions, any more than I know how and why my relationships with friends and lovers have survived the grinding wear and tear of such dark, fierce, and damaging energy. The aftermath of such violence, like the aftermath of a suicide attempt, is deeply bruising to all concerned. And, as with a suicide attempt, living with the knowledge that one has been violent forces a difficult reconciliation of totally divergent notions of oneself. After my suicide attempt, I had to reconcile my image of myself as a young girl who had been filled with enthusiasm, high hopes, great expectations, enormous energy, and dreams and love of life, with that of a dreary, crabbed, pained woman who desperately wished only for death and took a lethal dose of lithium in order to accomplish it. After each of my violent psychotic episodes, I had to try and reconcile my notion of myself as a reasonably quiet-spoken and highly disciplined person, one at least generally sensitive to the moods and feelings of others, with an enraged, utterly insane, and abusive woman who lost access to all control or reason.

These discrepancies between what one is, what one is brought up to believe is the right way of behaving toward others, and what actually happens during these awful black manias, or mixed states, are absolute and disturbing beyond description—particularly, I think, for a woman brought up in a highly conservative and traditional world. They seem a very long way from my mother's grace and gentleness, and farther still from the quiet seasons of cotillions, taffetas and silks, and elegant gloves that slid up over the elbows and had pearl buttons at the wrist, when one had no worries other than making sure that the seams in one's stockings were straight before going to Sunday-night dinners at the Officers' Club.

For the most important and shaping years of my life I had been brought up in a straitlaced world, taught to be thoughtful of others, circumspect, and restrained in my actions. We went as a family to church every Sunday, and all of my answers to adults ended with a "ma'am" or a "sir." The independence encouraged by my parents had been of an intellectual, not socially disruptive, nature. Then, suddenly, I was unpredictably and uncontrollably irrational and destructive. This was not something that could be overcome by protocol or etiquette. God, conspicuously, was nowhere to be found. Navy Cotillion, candy-striping, and *Tiffany's Table Manners for Teenagers* could not, nor were they ever intended to be, any preparation or match for madness. Uncontrollable anger and violence are dreadfully, irreconcilably, far from a civilized and predictable world.

I had, ever since I could remember, inclined in the direction of strong and exuberant feelings, loving and living with what Delmore Schwartz called "the throat of exaltation." Inflammability, however, always lay just the other side of exaltation. These fiery moods were, at least initially, not all bad: in addition to giving a certain romantic tumultuousness to my personal life, they had, over the years, added a great deal that was positive to my professional life. Certainly, they had ignited and propelled much of my writing, research, and advocacy work. They had driven me to try and make a difference. They had made me impatient with life as it was and made me restless for more. But, always, there was a lingering discomfort when the impatience or ardor or restlessness tipped over into too much anger. It did not seem consistent with being the kind of gentle, well-bred woman I had been brought up to admire and, indeed, continue to admire.

Depression, somehow, is much more in line with society's notions of what women are all about: passive, sensitive, hopeless, helpless, stricken, dependent, confused, rather tiresome, and with limited aspirations. Manic states, on the other hand, seem to be more the provenance of men: restless, fiery, aggressive, volatile, energetic, risk taking, grandiose and visionary, and impatient with the status quo. Anger or irritability in men, under such circumstances, is more tolerated and understandable; leaders or takers of voyages are permitted a wider latitude for being temperamental. Journalists and other writers, quite understandably, have tended to focus on women and depression, rather than women and mania. This is not surprising: depression is twice as common in women as men. But manic-depressive illness occurs equally often in women and men, and, being a relatively common condition, mania ends up affecting a large number of women. They, in turn, often are misdiagnosed, receive poor, if any, psychiatric treatment, and are at high risk for suicide, alcoholism, drug abuse, and violence. But they, like men who have manic-depressive illness, also often contribute a great deal of energy, fire, enthusiasm, and imagination to the people and world around them.

Manic-depression is a disease that both kills and gives life. Fire, by its nature, both creates and destroys. "The force that through the green fuse drives the flower," wrote Dylan Thomas, "Drives my green age; that blasts the roots of trees / Is my destroyer." Mania is a strange and driving force, a destroyer, a fire in the blood. Fortunately, having fire in one's blood is not without its benefits in the world of academic medicine, especially in the pursuit of tenure.

Tenure

*T*enure is the closest thing to a blood sport that first-class universities can offer: it is intensely competitive, all-consuming, exciting, fast, rather brutal, and very male. Pursuing tenure in a university medical school—where clinical responsibilities are layered upon the usual ones of research and teaching—ratchets up everything by several orders of magnitude. All things considered, being a woman, a nonphysician, and a manic-depressive was not the ideal way to start down the notoriously difficult road to tenure.

Obtaining tenure was not only a matter of academic and financial security for me. I had had, within months of starting as an assistant professor, my first episode of psychotic mania. The years leading up to tenure, which extended from 1974 to 1981, consisted of more than just the usual difficulties of competing in the very energetic and aggressive world of academic medicine. They were, more important, marked by struggles to stay sane, stay alive, and to come to terms with my illness. As the years went by I became more and more determined to pull out some good from all of the pain, to try and put my illness to some use. Tenure became a time of both possibility and transformation; it also became a symbol of the stability I craved and the ultimate recognition I sought for having competed and survived in the normal world.

After I was assigned to the adult inpatient service for my first teaching and clinical responsibilities, I soon grew restless, to say nothing of finding it increasingly difficult to keep a straight face while interpreting the psychological test results of patients from the ward. Trying to make sense out of Rorschach tests, which seemed a speculative venture on a good day, often made me feel as though I might as well be reading tarot cards or discussing the alignment of the planets. This was not why I had gotten a Ph.D., and I was beginning to understand Bob Dylan's lines "Twenty years of schoolin' and they put you on the day shift." Only it was twenty-three years, and I was still pulling a lot of night shift as well. My intellectual interests were widely and absurdly scattered during my early years on the faculty. I was, among other things, starting up a research project on hyraxes, elephants, and violence (a lingering remnant of the chancellor's garden party); writing up findings from the LSD, marijuana, and opiate studies I had done in graduate school; contemplating a study, to be done with my brother, that would examine the economics of dam-building behavior in beavers; conducting pain research and studies of phantom breast syndrome with my colleagues in the anesthesiology department; coauthoring an undergraduate textbook on abnormal psychology; acting as co-investigator on a study of the effects of marijuana on nausea and vomiting in cancer chemotherapy patients; and trying to figure out a legitimate way to do animal behavior studies at the Los Angeles Zoo. It was too much and too diffuse. My personal interests eventually forced me to focus on what I was doing and why. I gradually narrowed down my work to the study and treatment of mood disorders.

More specifically, and not surprisingly, I became particularly interested in manic-depressive illness. I was absolutely and single-mindedly determined to make a difference in how the illness was seen and treated. Two of my colleagues, both of whom had a great deal of clinical and research experience with mood disorders, and I decided to set up an outpatient clinic at UCLA that would specialize in the diagnosis and treatment of depression and manic-depressive illness. We received enough initial funding from the hospital to allow us to hire a nurse and buy some file cabinets. The medical director and I spent weeks developing diagnostic and research forms and then put together a teaching program that would qualify as a clinical rotation, or training experience, for third-year psychiatric residents and predoctoral psychology interns. Although there was some opposition to the fact that I, as a nonphysician, was the director of a medical clinic, most of the medical staff—especially the medical director of the clinic, the chairman of the psychiatry department, and the chief of staff of the Neuropsychiatric Institute—backed me up.

Within a few years, the UCLA Affective Disorders Clinic had become a large teaching and research facility. We evaluated and treated thousands of patients with mood disorders, carried out a large number of both medical and psychological research studies, and taught psychiatric residents and clinical psychology interns how to diagnose and take care of patients with mood disorders. The clinic became a popular choice for training. It was a scurrying, busy, emergency- and crisis-filled rotation due to the nature and severity of the illnesses being treated, but it also was generally a warm and laughter-filled place. The medical director and I encouraged not only hard work and long hours, but after-hour partying as well. The stress of treating suicidal, psychotic, and potentially violent patients was considerable for all of us, but we tried to back up the clinical responsibility carried by the interns and residents with as much supervision as possible. When the relatively rare catastrophe did occur—an extremely bright young lawyer, for example, refused all efforts to be hospitalized and then committed suicide by shooting himself through the head—the faculty, residents, and interns would meet, in small and larger groups, in order to figure out what had happened and to support not only the devastated family members, but the individuals who had borne the primary clinical responsibility. In the particular instance of the lawyer, the resident had done everything that anyone could possibly have been expected to do; not surprisingly, she was terribly shaken by his death. Ironically, it is usually those doctors who are the most competent and conscientious who feel the most sense of failure and pain.

We placed a strong emphasis upon the combined use of medications and psychotherapy, rather than medications alone, and stressed the importance of education about the illnesses and their treatments to patients and their families. My own experience as a patient had made me particularly aware of how critical psychotherapy could be in making some sense out of all the pain; how it could keep one alive long enough to have a chance at getting well; and how it could help one to learn to reconcile the resentments at taking medication with the terrible consequences of not taking it. In addition to the basics of teaching differential diagnosis, psychopharmacology, and other aspects of the clinical management of mood disorders, much of the teaching, clinical practice, and research revolved around a few central themes: why patients resist or refuse to take lithium and other medications; clinical states most likely to result in suicide, and how to mitigate them; the role of psychotherapy in the long-term outcome of depressive and manic-depressive illness; and the positive aspects of the illness that can arise during the milder manic states: heightened energy and perceptual awareness, increased fluidity and originality of thinking, intense exhilaration of moods and experience, increased sexual desire, expansiveness of vision, and a lengthened grasp of aspiration. I tried to encourage our clinic doctors to see that this was an illness that could confer advantage as well as disadvantage, and that for many individuals these intoxicating experiences were highly addictive in nature and difficult to give up.

In order to give the residents and interns some notion of the experiences that patients went through when manic and depressed, we encouraged them to read firsthand accounts from patients and writers who had suffered from mood disorders. I also started giving Christmas lectures to the house staff and clinic staff that focused on music written by composers who had experienced severe depression or manic-depressive illness.

These informal lectures became the basis for a concert that a friend of mine, a professor of music at UCLA, and I subsequently produced in 1985 with the Los Angeles Philharmonic. In an attempt to raise public awareness about mental illness, especially manic-depressive illness, we proposed to the executive director of the Philharmonic a program based on the lives and music of several composers who had suffered from the illness, including Robert Schumann, Hector Berlioz, and Hugo Wolf. The Philharmonic was enthusiastic, cooperative, and generous in the fees they negotiated. Unfortunately, a few days after I signed the contract, the University of California announced that it was beginning a major financial development campaign and that individual members of the faculty no longer would be able to solicit funds from private donors. I was left with a personal bill for twenty-five thousand dollars, which, as one of my friends pointed out, was a lot of money for concert tickets. Still, the concert filled UCLA's huge Royce Hall and was a great success; it also turned out to be the beginning of a series of concerts performed across the country, including one that we did a few years later with the National Symphony Orchestra at the John F. Kennedy Center for the Performing Arts in Washington, D.C. It was also the basis for the first of a series of public television specials that we produced around the theme of manic-depressive illness and the arts.

Throughout the setting up and running of the clinic I was fortunate to have the support of the chairman of my department. He backed my being director of a medical clinic despite the fact that I was not a physician, and despite the fact that he knew I had manic-depressive illness. Rather than using my illness as a reason to curtail my clinical and teaching responsibilities, he—after being assured that I was receiving good psychiatric care and that the medical director of the clinic knew about my condition—encouraged me to use it to try and develop better treatments and to help change public attitudes. Although he never said, I assume my chairman found out about my illness after my first episode of severe psychotic mania; my ward chief certainly knew, and I imagine that the information quickly drifted upward. In any event, my chairman treated the issue strictly as a medical one. He first broached the subject by coming up to me at a meeting, putting his arm around me, and saying, "I understand you have some problems with your moods. I'm sorry. For God's sake, just be sure to keep taking your lithium." Now and again, after that, he would ask me how I was doing and make sure that I was still taking my medication. He was straightforward, supportive, and never suggested for a moment that I stop or curtail my clinical work.

My concerns about openly discussing my illness with others, however, were enormous. My first psychotic episode occurred long before I received my license from the California Board of Medical Examiners. During the period of time between starting lithium and passing my written and oral board examinations, I observed many medical students, clinical psychology interns, and residents denied permission to continue their studies because of psychiatric illness. This happens far less often now—indeed, most graduate and medical schools encourage students who become ill to get treatment and, if at all possible, to return to their clinical work—but my early years on the faculty at UCLA were plagued by fears that my illness would be discovered, that I would be reported to one kind of hospital or licensing board or another, and that I would be required to give up my clinical practice and teaching.

It was a high-pressure existence in many ways, but mostly I loved it. Academic medicine provides an interesting and varied lifestyle, lots of travel, and most of one's colleagues are bright-eyed, bushy tailed, and generally thrive on the stresses of having to combine clinical practice with publishing papers and teaching. These stresses were compounded by the fluctuations in mood, however attenuated, that I continued to experience while on lithium. It took several years for them to truly even out. For me, when I was well, it was a wide-open opportunity to write, think, see patients, and teach. When I was ill, it was simply overwhelming: for days and weeks at a time, I would put up the DO NOT DISTURB sign on my door, stare mindlessly out the window, sleep, contemplate suicide, or watch my guinea pig—a memento of one of my manic buying sprees—furiously scurrying around in his cage. During those times I could not imagine writing another paper, and I was incapable of comprehending any of the journal articles that I would try to read. Supervising and teaching were ordeals.

But it was a tidal existence: When I was depressed, nothing came to me, and nothing came out of me. When manic, or mildly so, I would write a paper in a day, ideas would flow, I would design new studies, catch up on my patient charts and correspondence, and chip away at the mindless mounds of bureaucratic paperwork that defined the job of a clinic director. Like everything else in my life, the grim was usually set off by the grand; the grand, in turn, would yet again be canceled out by the grim. It was a loopy but intense life: marvelous, ghastly, dreadful, indescribably difficult, gloriously and unexpectedly easy, complicated, great fun, and a no-exit nightmare.

My friends, fortunately, were either a bit loopy themselves, or remarkably tolerant of the chaos that formed the basic core of my emotional existence. I spent a great deal of time with them during those assistant-professorship years. I also traveled frequently, for business and pleasure, and played squash with interns, friends, and colleagues. Sports were fun only up to a point, however, as lithium threw off my coordination. This was true not only for squash, but particularly for riding horses; I finally had to stop riding for several years, after falling off one too many times while jumping. I can look back now and think that perhaps all of that wasn't so bad, but, in fact, each time I had to give up a sport I had to give up not only the fun of that sport, but also that part of myself that I had known as an athlete. Manic-depressive illness forces one to deal with many aspects of growing old—with its physical and mental infirmities—many decades in advance of age itself.

Life in the fast track, the dashing about and scrambling for tenure and for recognition from one's peers, continued at a frenetic pace. When I was manic, the tempo seemed slow; when I was normal, frenetic seemed fine; when I was depressed, the pace was impossible. Other than my psychiatrist, there was no one I could talk to about the real extent of the difficulties I was having. Or perhaps there was, but it never really occurred to me to try. There were next to no other women in the adult psychiatry division; the women that did exist in the department all clumped together in child psychiatry. They were no protection against the weasels in the woodwork, and, besides, they had weasels enough in their own quarters. Although most of my male colleagues were fair, and many were exceptionally supportive, there were several men whose views of women had to be experienced to be believed.

The Oyster was one such man, one such experience. Named for his smooth and slithery essence, the Oyster was a senior professor: he was patronizing, smug, and had all of the intellectual and emotional complexity of, as one might expect, a small mollusk. He thought of women in terms of breasts, not minds, and it always seemed to irritate him that most women had both. He also thought women who strayed into academic medicine were fundamentally flawed, and, as I was particularly disinclined to be deferential, I seemed especially to annoy him. We served together on the Appointments and Promotions Committee for the department, where I was the only woman among the eighteen members. On the occasions when he would actually show up for meetings—the Oyster was notorious for earning a maximum amount of money for spending a minimum amount of time in the hospital— I would try to sit directly across the table from him and watch his failed attempts to be unfailingly polite.

I always had the sense that he thought I was a bit of a mutant but, because I was not absolutely hideous, that I might yet be saved by a good marriage. I, for my part, would randomly congratulate him on his efforts to recruit more women into the department. His lack of gray matter was ably matched by his lack of wit, and, as he of course had never made any attempts whatsoever in that direction, he would look suspiciously in my direction and then dart me a baffled and irritated smile. He would have been likably goofy except that he had real power in the department, and he made clear his views about women every step of the way: his sexual innuendos were deeply offensive, and his level of condescension whenever he spoke with me, or women interns and residents, was infuriating. He was a caricature of himself, in many ways, but it was clear that being a woman on his service meant starting ten seconds late for a hundred-yard dash. Fortunately, the tenure process has many checks and balances built into it, and, at least in the two universities that I know best—the University of California and Johns Hopkins—the system seems to me to be a remarkably fair one. Entities like the Oyster didn't make it any easier, however.

Finally, after much rodenting along and through the tenure maze, I received my letter from the regents notifying me that I had been promoted to the next set of academic mazes: the holding pattern, the Inferno-land of Associate Professordom. I celebrated for weeks. One of my best friends had a lovely dinner party for about thirty people, on a perfect California night; the terraces in her gardens were filled with flowers and candles; it could not have been more beautiful. My family provided the champagne, along with their gift to me of Baccarat glasses for the champagne, and I had a wonderful time. More than anyone, my family and friends knew how much the tenure party was a celebration over years of struggling against severe mental illness, as well as a celebration of the major rite of academic passage.

Tenure really sank in, however, when one of my colleagues, a member of the all-male Bohemian Club, came over to my house with some wine from his club. "Congratulations, Professor," he said, handing me the bottle. "Welcome to an all-men's club."

Part Three

THIS MEDICINE, LOVE

An Officer
and a Gentleman

There was a time when I honestly believed that there was only a certain amount of pain one had to go through in life. Because manic-depressive illness had brought such misery and uncertainty in its wake, I presumed life should therefore be kinder to me in other, more balancing ways. But then I also had believed that I could fly through starfields and slide along the rings of Saturn. Perhaps my judgment left something to be desired. Robert Lowell, often crazy but rarely stupid, knew better than to assume a straight shot at happiness: If we see a light at the end of the tunnel, he said, it's the light of an oncoming train.

For a while—courtesy of lithium, time's passing, and the love of a tall, handsome Englishman—I caught a glimpse of what I imagined to be the light at the end of the tunnel, and I could feel, however elusively, what seemed to be the return of a warm and secure existence. I learned how marvelously the mind can heal, given half a chance, and how patience and gentleness can put back together the pieces of a horribly shattered world. What God had put asunder, an elemental salt, a first-rank psychiatrist, and a man's kindness and love could put almost right again.

I met David my first year on the faculty at UCLA. It was early in 1975, six months after I had gone barkingly manic, and my brain had gradually knit itself into a rather brittle, but vaguely coherent, version of its former self. My mind was skating on thin ice, my emotions were completely frayed, and most of my true existence was lived within the narrow range of very long-cast inner shadows. But my overt actions were within the conservative range of my so-called normal colleagues, so—at least professionally speaking—all was ostensibly well.

On this particular day I had unlocked the door to the inpatient ward with my usual sense of annoyance—not because of the patients, but because there was a staff meeting scheduled, which meant that the nurses would be venting their collective spleen on the psychiatric residents, who would, in turn, be irritatingly secure in their knowledge that they had the final authority and higher degrees; the ward chief, who was hopelessly ineffectual, would allow the resentments, envies, and personal animosities to completely dominate the meetings. Patient care, on that particular ward, often took a backseat to staff neuroses, internecine wars, and self-indulgence. Having procrastinated as long as I could, I walked into the conference room, looked for a chair out of the line of fire, and sat down to see how the inevitable unpleasantries would unfold.

To my amazement, the ward psychiatrist came in accompanied by a very tall, good-looking man who looked at me and smiled wonderfully. He turned out to be a visiting professor, a psychiatrist on leave from the Royal Army Medical Corps, and we liked one another immediately. That afternoon we had a cup of coffee together in the hospital cafeteria, and I found myself opening up to him in a way that I hadn't done in a very long time. He was soft-spoken, quiet and thoughtful, and didn't push too hard against the edges of my still very raw soul. We both loved music and poetry; had military backgrounds in common; and, because I had studied in Scotland and England, had common experiences of cities, hospitals, and countrysides as well. He was interested in learning about the differences between British and American psychiatric practices, so I asked him to consult on one of my most difficult patients, a schizophrenic girl who believed she was a witch. He quickly saw through to the medical and psychotherapeutic issues that had been so slow to come out of her guarded and frightened mind. He was unbelievably kind to her, while remaining very much a doctor, and she sensed—as I did later—that she could trust him implicitly. His manner was matter-of-fact, but warm, and I enjoyed watching him gently phrase and then rephrase questions so as to win her trust and reach beyond her paranoia.

David and I frequently had lunch together during his months at UCLA, often in the university's botanical gardens. He repeatedly asked me to dinner, and I, as repeatedly, said I could not because I was still married and again living with my husband, after our initial separation. He returned to London, and, although we wrote to one another occasionally, I was preoccupied with teaching, running a clinic, getting tenure, problems in my marriage, and another bad attack of mania, which, as day the night, was followed by a long, absolutely paralyzing depression.

My husband and I, although we had remained close friends and saw one another often, finally decided that our marriage was beyond the point of repair. I don't think it ever really had a chance after I had impulsively left during my first manic episode. But we both tried. We talked a lot, and we discussed our mistakes and possibilities over many a meal and glass of wine. There was a great deal of goodwill and caring, but nothing could put our marriage back together after all that had happened in the wake of my illness. Somewhere in the midst of all of this, I wrote to David that I had again and finally separated from my husband. Life went on, a blur of clinic meetings, writing papers, seeing patients, and teaching residents, interns, and graduate students. I lived in terror that someone would find out how ill I had been, how fragile I still was, but—oddly and fortunately—sensitivity and keen observation are not always the long suits of academic psychiatrists.

Then one day, more than eighteen months after he had left UCLA, I returned to my office to find David sitting in my chair, playing with a pencil, and smiling broadly. He said, half laughing, "Surely you'll have dinner with me now. I've waited a long time and come a long way." I did, of course, and we had several marvelous days in Los Angeles before he returned to England. He asked me to come stay with him for a few weeks in London. Although I was still recovering from a long suicidal depression, and my thoughts were so halting and my feelings so gray I could scarcely bear it, I somehow knew that things would be made better by being with him. They were. Immeasurably. We had long,

late-spring evening walks in St. James's Park, dinner at
his club overlooking the Thames, and picnics in Hyde
Park, which was just across the street from his flat. Gradually the exhaustion, wariness, and black faithlessness
lifted. I began to enjoy music and paintings again, to
laugh again, to write poetry again. Long nights and
early mornings of incredible passion made me again
believe in, or remember, how important a sense of life
is to love, and love to life.

David worked at the hospital during the days so I
reinvolved myself in the London I had once cared so
much about. I went for long walks in the parks, visited
and revisited the Tate, wandered aimlessly around the
Victoria and Albert, as well as the Natural History and
Science Museums. One day, on David's suggestion, I
took the boat from Westminster Pier to Greenwich and
back; another day I took the train to Canterbury. I
hadn't been to Canterbury in years and had seen it only,
but unforgettably, through rather manic eyes. I had
long-lasting, mystical memories of the dark gorgeous
stained glass, the chilled sounds, the simple, grim place
of Becket's murder, and the intense, transient light
patterns on the cathedral floor. This time, however, I
kneeled without ecstasy, prayed without belief, and felt
as a stranger. It was, all the same, a quieter and gentler
sense of Canterbury that I got.

In the midst of this godless kneeling, I suddenly
remembered that I had forgotten to take my lithium the
night before. I reached into my purse for my medication, opened the bottle, and immediately dropped all of
the pills onto the cathedral floor. The floor was filthy,
there were people all around, and I was too embarrassed
to bend over and pick up the pills. It was a moment not

only of embarrassment, but of reckoning as well; it meant I would have to ask David to write a prescription for me, and that meant, of course, that I would have to tell him about my illness. I couldn't help thinking, with more than a trace of bitterness, that God seldom opens one door that he doesn't close another. However, I couldn't afford not to obtain new medication: the last time I had stopped my lithium I had gotten manic almost immediately. I could not survive another year like the one I had just been through.

That night, before we went to bed, I told David about my manic-depressive illness. I dreaded what his reaction would be and was furious with myself for not having told him earlier. He was silent for a very long time, and I could see that he was sorting through all of the implications, medical and personal, of what I had just said. I had no doubt he loved me, but he knew as well as I did how uncertain the course of the illness could be. He was an army officer, his family was extremely conservative, he desperately wanted children, and manic-depressive illness was hereditary. It also was not talked about. It was unpredictable, and not uncommonly fatal. I wished I had never told him; I wished I was normal, wished I was anywhere but where I was. I felt like an idiot for hoping that anyone could accept what I had just said and resigned myself to a subtle round of polite farewells. We were not married, after all, nor had we been seriously involved for any extended time.

Finally, after eternity had ticked to a close, David turned to me, put his arms around me, and said softly, "I say. *Rotten* luck." I was overcome with relief; I also was struck by the absolute truth of what he just had said. It *was* rotten luck, and somebody finally understood. All the while, in the midst of my relief, the small, shredded island of humor that remained in my mind, recorded, on a totally different brain track, that David's phrasing sounded like something straight out of a P. G. Wodehouse novel. I told him this and reminded him of the Wodehouse character who complained that while it was true that he wasn't disgruntled, he wasn't altogether gruntled either. We both laughed for a long time, somewhat nervously to be sure, but some of the awful ice was broken.

David could not have been kinder or more accepting; he asked me question after question about what I had been through, what had been most terrible, what had frightened me the most, and what he could do to help me when I was ill. Somehow, after that conversation, everything became easier for me: I felt, for the first time, that I was not alone in dealing with all of the pain and uncertainty, and it was clear to me that he genuinely wanted to understand my illness and to take care of me. He started that night. I explained to him that, due to the relatively rare side effects of lithium that affected both my vision and concentration, I essentially could not read more than a paragraph or two at a time. So he read to me: he read poetry, Wilkie Collins, and Thomas Hardy, with one arm around me in bed, smoothing my hair now and again, as though I were a child. Moment by moment, with infinite patience and tact, his gentleness—and his belief in me, in who I was, and in my basic health—pushed back the nightmare fears of unpredictable moods and violence.

It must have been clear to David that I despaired of ever returning to my normal self, because he set about, in his rather systematic way, to reassure me. The next evening, when he came home, he announced that he had arranged dinner invitations from two senior British army officers, both of whom had manic-depressive illness. The evenings that we spent with these two men and their wives were unforgettable. One of the men, a general, was elegant, charming, and very smart; his lucidity was beyond question. He was—other than an occasional restlessness in his eyes and a slightly melancholic, albeit savingly sardonic, tinge to his conversation—indistinguishable from the animated, self-assured, and entertaining types one encounters at London and Oxford dinner parties. The other officer was also wonderful—warm, witty, and, like the general, had a "frightfully, frightfully" upper-crust accent. He, too, had an occasional sad aspect to his eyes, but he was terrific company and has remained, over many years, a close friend.

At no time during either of the dinner parties was manic-depressive illness discussed; it was, in fact, the very normality of the evenings that was so reassuring and so important to me. Being introduced to such "normal" men, both from a world much like the one I had known as a child, was one of David's many intuitive acts of kindness. "It is the history of our kindnesses that alone makes this world tolerable," wrote Robert Louis Stevenson. "If it were not for that, for the effect of kind words, kind looks, kind letters . . . I should be inclined to think our life a practical jest in the worst possible spirit." After knowing David, I never again saw life in its worst possible spirit.

I left London with a terrible sense of apprehension, but David wrote and called often. In the late fall we spent time together in Washington, and, as I finally was feeling myself again, I enjoyed life in ways that I hadn't for years. Those November days remain in my memory as a gentle yet intensely romantic swirl of long walks in the cold, visits to old houses and yet older churches, light snows covering the eighteenth-century gardens of Annapolis, and icy rivers threading their way out of and beyond the Chesapeake Bay. The evenings were filled with dry sherry and meandering dinner conversations about almost everything; the nights were filled with wonderful lovemaking and much-sought, long-absent, untroubled sleep.

David returned to London; I returned to Los Angeles; we wrote and spoke often, missed one another, and threw ourselves into our respective lives of work. I went back to England in May, and we had two weeks of long, warm pre-summer days in London, Dorset, and Devon. One Sunday morning, after church, we walked up into the hills to listen to the ringing of the church bells, and I noticed that David had stopped, was standing still, and breathing heavily. He joked about getting too much strenuous exercise at night, we both laughed, and left it at that.

David was posted to the British Army Hospital in Hong Kong, and he made plans for me to visit him there. He wrote in detail about the evening events he had arranged for us, the people he wanted me to meet, and the picnics we would take to the islands nearby. I could not wait to be with him again. But then one night, not too long before I was to join him, I was at home writing a chapter for a textbook when there was a knock at my door. It was an odd hour, I was expecting no one, and for some even odder reason I suddenly remembered what my mother had said about how pilots' wives dreaded the chaplain's knock on the door. I opened the door, and it was a diplomatic courier with a letter from David's commanding officer saying that David, who had been on general medical duty in Kathmandu, had died very suddenly of a massive heart attack. He was forty-four, and I was thirty-two.

Very little sank in. I remember sitting down, picking up my work again, writing for a while, and then telephoning my mother. I spoke also with David's parents and his commanding officer. Even when we were discussing plans for the funeral, which was significantly delayed because the army required an autopsy before David's body could be returned to England, his death in no way seemed real to me. I went through all of the motions in a state of complete shock—I booked a flight, taught my seminar the next morning, ran a clinic staff meeting, renewed my passport, packed my clothes, and carefully gathered up all of David's letters to me. Once I was on the airplane, I methodically put the letters into order according to when they had been written; I decided to wait until I got to London, however, before reading them. The next day, in Hyde Park, when I sat down to read, I found I could get through only the first half of the first letter. I started sobbing uncontrollably. To this day I have neither reopened nor reread any of his letters.

I found my way to Harrods to pick out a black hat for the funeral and then had lunch with David's commanding officer at his club. He was, by virtue of his job, chief psychiatrist for the British army; by temperament, he was kind, direct, and tremendously understanding. He was used to dealing with women whose husbands had died unexpectedly, knew desperate denial when he saw it, and clearly grasped that I had not even begun to comprehend the reality of David's death. He talked to me for a long time about David, about the many years he had known and worked with him, and what a wonderful doctor and person he had been. He also said he thought it might be "terribly difficult, but a good idea" if he read me portions of the autopsy report. Ostensibly, this was to reassure me that the massiveness of David's heart attack was such that no treatment or medical intervention would have helped. In actuality, it was clear he knew that the cold-blooded medical language would shock me into beginning to deal with the finality of it all. It certainly helped, although it was not so much the gruesome medical details that lurched me toward reality; it was, instead, the brigadier's statement that "a young officer had accompanied the body of Colonel Laurie on the Royal Air Force plane from Hong Kong to Brize Norton airfield." David no longer was Colonel Laurie; he no longer was Dr. Laurie; he was a body.

The British army was unbelievably kind to me. By definition the army is used to death, especially sudden death, and much that is healing comes from their traditions. The rituals of military funerals are in themselves predictable, reassuring, dignified, religious, and dreadfully final. David's friends and fellow officers were blunt, witty, matter-of-fact, and deeply compassionate. They made clear the expectation that I would handle things well, but they also did every conceivable thing possible to make a terrible situation more bearable. They never left me alone, but they never hovered; they kept me plied with sherry and scotch; they offered me legal counsel. They frequently, openly, and humorously discussed David; they left little room for denial.

During the funeral itself, the brigadier insisted I sing along with the hymns, kept his arm around me during particularly difficult times, and laughed out loud when I whispered to him, during a somewhat overdone eulogy about officers and gentlemen, that I wished I could just get up and say that David had been great in bed. Despite my revulsion at the grotesque reduction of a man who had been six feet three inches tall into a small box of ashes, and an overwhelming desire to stay back from the grave site, he again pushed me forward to watch, to take it in, to believe it to be so.

I spent the rest of my time in England with friends and, bit by bit, began to understand that the future I had assumed, and the love and support I had come to depend upon, were gone. There were a thousand things I remembered once David had died. And there were many, many regrets: for lost opportunities, unnecessary and damaging arguments, and a deepening realization that there was absolutely nothing that could be done to change that which was true. There were so many dreams lost: all of our plans for a house full of children were lost; all of seemingly everything was lost. But grief, fortunately, is very different from depression: it is sad, it is awful, but it is not without hope. David's death did not plunge me into unendurable darkness; suicide never crossed my mind. And there was very real solace in the offsetting and enormous kindness of friends, family, and even strangers. The day I left England to return to America, for instance, an agent at the British Airways ticket counter asked me if my trip had been for business or holiday. My composure, which had been airtight for almost two weeks, suddenly snapped. I explained, through a flood of tears, the circumstances of my visit; the agent immediately upgraded my seat and put me where I could have as much privacy as possible. He must have sent the word ahead to the stewardesses, because they too were unusually kind, solicitous, and left me to my thoughts. Since that day, whenever possible, I fly British Airways. And, each time, I am reminded of the importance of small kindnesses.

I returned home to a tremendous amount of work, which was genuinely helpful, and, unnervingly, to several letters from David, which had arrived in my absence. In the days to follow I received two other letters, long delayed in the mail, and then, inevitably and terribly, they stopped. The shock of David's death gradually disappeared over time. Missing him never has. Several years after his death I was asked to speak about it. I ended with a poem written by Edna St. Vincent Millay:

> *Time does not bring relief; you all have lied*
> *Who told me time would ease me of my pain!*
> *I miss him in the weeping of the rain;*
> *I want him at the shrinking of the tide;*
> *The old snows melt from every mountain-side,*
> *And last year's leaves are smoke in every lane;*

But last year's bitter loving must remain
Heaped on my heart, and my old thoughts abide.
There are a hundred places where I fear
To go,—so with his memory they brim.
And entering with relief some quiet place
Where never fell his foot or shone his face
I say, "There is no memory of him here!"
And so stand stricken, so remembering him.

Time finally did bring relief. But it took its own, and not terribly sweet, time in doing so.

They Tell Me
It Rained

The accumulated pain and uncertainty from David's death, as well as from my own illness, for several years very much lowered and narrowed my expectations of life. I drew into myself and, for all intents and purposes, shuttered my heart from any unnecessary exposure to the world. I worked hard. Running a clinic, teaching, doing research, and writing books were no substitute for love, but they were interesting and gave some meaning to my badly interrupted life. Having finally cottoned onto the disastrous consequences of starting and stopping lithium, I took it faithfully and found that life was a much stabler and more predictable place than I had ever reckoned. My moods were still intense and my temperament rather quick to the boil, but I could make plans with far more certainty and the periods of absolute blackness were fewer and less extreme.

Still, I was unquestionably raw and unhealed inside. At no point in the eight years since I had joined the faculty—despite the repeated, long months of manias and depressions, my suicide attempt, and David's death—had I taken off any extended time from work, or away from Los Angeles, in order to heal and bind up the massive and long-standing wounds. So dipping into that most fabulous of all professorial perks, I decided to take a year's sabbatical leave in England. Like St. Andrews many years before, it turned out to be a gentle and wonderful interlude. Love, long periods of time to myself, and a marvelous life in London and Oxford gave both my mind and heart the chance to slowly put back together most of that which had been ripped apart.

My academic reasons for going to England were to conduct a study of mood disorders in eminent British artists and writers and to work on a medical text about manic-depressive illness that I was writing with a colleague. My time was split between work at St. George's Hospital Medical School in London and the University of Oxford. They could not have been more different experiences, each wonderful in very different ways. St. George's, a large teaching hospital now in the middle of one of London's poorest neighborhoods, was active and lively in the way that good teaching hospitals tend to be. It was 250 years old and had been home to Edward Jenner, the great surgeon John Hunter, and many other clinicians and scientists famous in the history of medicine; the hospital was also the final resting place for Blossom, the cow that Jenner had used in carrying out his smallpox vaccine research. Her somewhat mangy but magnificent hide hung under glass in the medical school library. When I first saw it, at a distance and without my glasses, I thought it was a strange and oddly beautiful abstract painting. I was delighted when I found out it was actually the hide of a cow, and not that of just any cow, but such a medically famous one. There was something very nice about working near Blossom, and I spent many happy hours in her company, working, or thinking about working, and looking up now and again at her motley but charming remains.

Oxford was totally different. I was a senior research fellow of Merton College, one of the three original Oxford colleges founded in the thirteenth century. Merton's chapel had been built during the same period, and some of its incredibly beautiful, deeply stained glass windows date from then as well. The library, built a century later and one of the finest medieval libraries in England, was also the first to house books upright on shelves instead of keeping them flat in chests. Its collection of early printed books is said to have been hampered by the fact that the college was convinced that the printing press was only a passing fad, one that would never be able to replace handwritten manuscripts. Some of that extraordinary confidence—so unburdened by either the realities of the present or the approaching of the future—still seeps through the Oxford colleges, creating, variously, annoyance or amusement, depending upon one's mood and circumstance.

I had a lovely suite of rooms at Merton overlooking the playing fields, and I read (albeit with difficulty) and wrote in total peace, interrupted only by a college servant who brought coffee in the mornings and tea in the afternoons. Lunch was almost always with the senior fellows, a remarkably interesting, if occasionally odd, group of senior lecturers and professors representing all fields of study within the university. There were historians, mathematicians, philosophers, and literary scholars, but whenever possible I would sit next to Sir Alister Hardy, the marine biologist, who was a fascinating man and an extraordinary storyteller; I listened for hours to his accounts of his early scientific explorations to Antarctica, as well as his discussions of his ongoing research into the nature of religious experiences. We shared strong common interests in William James and the nature of ecstatic experiences, and he leapfrogged fields, from literature to biology to theology, without effort or pause.

Merton was not only among the oldest and wealthiest of the Oxford colleges, it was also widely acclaimed for having the best food and the finest wine cellar. For that reason, I not infrequently found myself in Oxford for college dinners. Those evenings were evenings far far back in time: sipping sherry and talking with the dons before dinner began; walking together, in procession, into the old and beautiful dining hall; watching with amusement as the black-gowned, scraggly undergraduates rose to their feet as the dons came in (the deference had a certain appeal; curtsying, perhaps, was not such a bad thing after all). Heads bowed, quick prayers in Latin, students and dons alike, we all would wait for the college warden to sit; this then, would be followed by an immediate and overpowering din of undergraduates scuffling with chairs, laughing, and shouting loudly up and down the long dining tables.

At the high table, the conversations and enthusiasm were more restrained, and, always, there was vintage Oxfordtalk, usually clever, often hilarious, occasionally stifling; excellent dinners with superb wines were all noted on elegantly calligraphied and crested menus; then we filed out into a smaller, private dining room for brandies and ports and fruit and candied ginger with the warden and fellows. I cannot imagine how anyone got any work done after these dinners, but, as everyone I met who taught at Oxford seemed to have written at least four definitive books on one obscure topic or another, they must have inherited, or cultivated, very different kinds of livers and brains. For my part, the wine and port would inevitably catch up with me, and, after pouring myself onto the last train to London, I would stare out of the window into the night, caught up, for an hour or so, in other centuries, and happily lost between worlds and eras.

Although I went to Oxford several times a week, most of my life was centered in London. I spent great and vastly enjoyable amounts of time wandering through parks and museums and took long weekends with friends who lived in East Sussex, walking along the downs overlooking the English Channel. I also started riding again. I felt the return of an amazing sense of life and vitality when taking a horse out through the misty mornings of Hyde Park during the cold, late autumn, and even more so galloping pell-mell over the Somerset countryside, through beech woods and across farmlands. I had forgotten what it felt like to be that open to wind and rain and beauty, and I could feel life seeping back into crevices of my body and mind that I had completely written off as dead or dormant.

It took my year in England to make me realize how much I had been simply treading water, settling on surviving and avoiding pain rather than being actively involved in and seeking out life. The chance to escape from the reminders of illness and death, from a hectic life, and from clinical and teaching responsibilities was not unlike my earlier year as an undergraduate in St. Andrews: it gave me a semblance of peace that had eluded me, and a place of my own to heal and mull, but most important to heal. England did not have the Celtic, magical quality of St. Andrews—nothing, I suppose, ever could for me—but it gave me back myself again, gave me back my high hopes of life. And it gave me back my belief in love.

I had come at last to some sort of terms with David's death. Visiting his grave in Dorset one cold, sunny day, I was taken aback by the loveliness of the churchyard in which he was buried. I had not remembered very much of it from the funeral, and certainly not its tranquillity and beauty. The deathly quietness was a certain kind of consolation, I suppose, but not necessarily the kind one would seek. I put a bouquet of long-stemmed violets on his grave and sat, tracing the letters of his name in the granite, remembering our times together in England and Washington and Los Angeles. It seemed a very long time ago, but I could see him still, tall and handsome, standing, arms crossed and laughing, at the top of a hill, during one of our walks in the English countryside; I still could feel his presence next to mine, kneeling together in a strange intimacy, at the communion rail in St. Paul's; and I still could feel, with absolute clarity, his arms tight around me, holding the world at bay, giving me comfort and safety in the midst of total desolation. I wished more than anything that he could see that I was well, and that I somehow could repay him for his kindness and his belief in me. But mostly, as I was sitting there in the graveyard, I thought of all of the things that David had missed by dying young. And then, after an hour or more of being lost in my thoughts, I was caught up short by the realization that I had been thinking, for the first time, about how much David had missed, rather than what we together would miss.

David had loved and accepted me in an extraordinary way; his steadiness and kindness had sustained and saved me, but he was gone. Life—because of him, and despite his death—went on. And now, four years after his death, I found a very different kind of love and a renewed belief in life. These came by way of an elegant, moody, and totally charming Englishman whom I had met early in the year. We both knew that, due to personal and professional circumstances, our affair would have to end once the year did, but it was—despite or because of this—a relationship that succeeded, finally, in restoring love and laughter and desire to a walled-in life and a thoroughly iced heart.

We had first met at a London dinner party during one of my earlier visits to England; it was, wonderfully, and without question, love at first sight. Neither of us had any awareness of anyone else at the dinner table that night, and neither of us—we agreed much later— had ever been so completely and irrationally swept away by the power of our feelings. Several months later, when I returned to London for my year's sabbatical leave, he called and asked me to go out to dinner. I was renting a mews house in South Kensington, so we went to a restaurant nearby. It was, for both of us, a continuation of what we had felt when we first met. I was spellbound by the ease with which he understood me, and physically overwhelmed by his intensity. We both knew, long before the wine was through, that we were beyond any way of turning back.

It was raining when we left the restaurant, and he put

his arm around me as we ran madcap to my place. Once there, he held me very close to him for a long, long time. I felt and smelled the rain against his coat, felt his arms around me, and remembered, with relief, how extraordinary scents and rain and love and life can be. I had not been with a man in a very long time, and, understanding this, he was kind and gentle and utterly loving. We saw each other as often as we could. Because we both were inclined to intense feelings and moods, we could console one another easily and, likewise, give one another a wide berth whenever necessary. We talked about everything. He was almost frighteningly intuitive, smart, passionate, and, occasionally, deeply melancholic; and he came to know me better than anyone had ever known me. He had no difficulty seeing the complexity in emotional situations or moods—his own made him well able to understand and respect irrationality, wild enthusiasms, paradox, change, and contradiction. We shared a love for poetry, music, tradition, and irreverence, as well as an unflagging awareness of the darker side of almost everything that was light, and the lighter side of almost everything that was bleak or morbid.

We created our own world of discussion, desire, and love, living on champagne, roses, snow, rain, and borrowed time, an intense and private island of restored life for both of us. I had no hesitancy in telling him everything about myself, and he, like David, was extremely understanding about my manic-depressive illness. His immediate response, after I told him, was to take my face in his hands, kiss me gently on either cheek, and say, "I thought it was impossible for me to love you any more than I do." He was silent for a while and then added, "It doesn't really surprise me, but it does explain

a certain vulnerability that goes along with your bold-
ness. I am very glad you told me." He meant it. They
were not just easy words to cover awkward feelings.
Everything he did and said after our discussion only
underscored the meaning of his words. He understood,
took into account, and put into perspective my vulner-
abilities; but he also knew and loved my strengths as he
saw them. He kept both in mind, protecting me from
the hurt and pain of my illness and loving those aspects
of me that he felt carried over with passion into life and
love and work and people.

I told him about my problems with the idea of taking lithium, but also that my life was dependent upon it.
I told him that I had discussed with my psychiatrist the
possibility of taking a lower dose in hopes of alleviating
some of the more problematic side effects; I was eager
to do this, but very frightened that I would have a
recurrence of my mania. He argued that there would
never be a safer or more protected period of time in my
life in which to do it and that he would see me
through. After discussing it with my psychiatrist in Los
Angeles and my doctor in London, I did, very slowly,
cut back on the amount of lithium I was taking. The
effect was dramatic. It was as though I had taken ban-
dages off my eyes after many years of partial blindness.
A few days after lowering my dose, I was walking in
Hyde Park, along the side of the Serpentine, when I
realized that my steps were literally bouncier than they
had been and that I was taking in sights and sounds that
previously had been filtered through thick layers of
gauze. The quacking of the ducks was more insistent,
clearer, and more intense; the bumps on the sidewalk
were far more noticeable; I felt more energetic and

alive. Most significant, I could once again read without effort. It was, in short, remarkable.

That night, waiting for my moody, intense Englishman to appear—needlepointing, watching the snow fall, listening to Chopin and Elgar—I suddenly was aware of how clear and poignant the music seemed, how intensely, beautifully melancholic it was to watch the snow and wait for him. I was feeling more beauty, but more real sadness as well. When he arrived—elegant, just in from a formal dinner party, black tie, white silk evening scarf draped, askew, around his neck, a bottle of champagne in his hand—I put on Schubert's posthumous Piano Sonata in B-flat, D. 960. Its haunting, beautiful eroticism absolutely filled me with emotion and made me weep. I wept for the poignancy of all the intensity I had lost without knowing it, and I wept for the pleasure of experiencing it again. To this day, I cannot hear that piece of music without feeling surrounded by the beautiful sadness of that evening, the love I was privileged to know, and the recollection of the precarious balance that exists between sanity and a subtle, dreadful muffling of the senses.

Once, after several days completely to ourselves and with no contact at all with the outside world, he brought me an anthology of writings about love. He had tagged one short entry that captured the essence not only of those intense, glorious days but of the entire year as well:

Thank you for a lovely weekend.
They tell me it rained.

Love Watching Madness

I dreaded leaving England.
My moods had held at a more even keel for longer than
I could remember; my heart was newly alive; and my
mind was in a glorious state, having loped, grazed, and
mulled its less medicated self through Oxford and St.
George's. It was increasingly hard to imagine giving up
the gentle pace of days I had set for myself in London,
and harder still to think of losing the passion and close
understanding that had filled my nights. England had
laid to rest most of my incessant wondering about the
what-ifs and whys and what-might-have-beens; it also
had laid to rest, in a very different way, my relentless
warrings with lithium, most of which had been nothing
but a futile battle against the givens of my own mind.
These warrings had cost me dearly in time lost, and,
feeling myself again, I was unwilling to risk losing any
more time than I already had. Life had become worth
not losing.

Inevitably, the year passed: the snows and warming
brandies of the English winter gave way to the soft rains

and white wines of early summer. Roses and horses appeared in Hyde Park; gorgeous, diaphanous apple blossoms spread out over the black branches of the trees in St. James's Park; and the long, still hours of summer light cast an Edwardian hue over the days just up to my parting. It had become difficult to remember my life in Los Angeles, much less to think about returning to the chaotic days of running a large university clinic filled with very sick patients, teaching, and seeing a full caseload of patients again. I was beginning to have doubts that I could remember the details of conducting a psychiatric history and examination, much less teaching others how to do it. I was reluctant to leave England, and even more reluctant to return to a city I had come to associate not only with a grueling academic career, but also with breakdowns, the worn, cold, bloodlessness following in their wake, and the draining charade of pretending to be well when I wasn't and going through the motions of being pleasant when I felt dreadful.

I was, however, very wrong in my forebodings. The year had served as far more than just a restful interlude; it had been, in fact, truly restorative. Teaching was once again fun; supervising the clinical work of the residents and interns was, as it had been in earlier times, a pleasure; and seeing patients gave me the opportunity to try to put into practice some of what I had learned from my own experiences. Mental exhaustion had taken a long, terrible toll, but, strangely, it was only in feeling well, energetic, and high-spirited again that I had any true sense of the toll taken.

So work went well and relatively smoothly. Much of my time was spent working on a textbook that I was coauthoring about manic-depressive illness, delighted with how much easier it was to read, analyze, and retain the medical literature, which, until only recently, had been a terrible struggle to comprehend. I found writing my sections of the textbook a satisfying mix of science, clinical medicine, and personal experience. I was concerned that these experiences might unduly influence—by content or emphasis—portions of what I wrote, but my coauthor was fully aware of my illness, and many other clinicians and scientists also reviewed what we wrote. Often, though, I found myself drawing upon certain aspects of what I had been through in order to emphasize a particular point of phenomenology or clinical practice. Many of the chapters I wrote—those about suicide, medication compliance, childhood and adolescence, psychotherapy, clinical description, creativity, personality and interpersonal behavior, thought disorder, perception, and cognition—were influenced by my strong belief that these were areas that had been relatively overlooked in the field. Others—such as epidemiology, alcohol and drug abuse, and assessment of manic and depressive states—were more straightforwardly a review of the existing psychiatric literature.

For the clinical description chapter—the basic characterization of hypomanic and manic states, depressive and mixed states, as well as the cyclothymic features underlying these clinical conditions—I relied not only upon the work of classic clinicians such as Professor Emil Kraepelin, and the many clinical researchers who had conducted extensive data-based studies, but upon the writings of manic-depressive patients themselves. Many of the descriptions were from writers and artists who had given highly articulate and vivid descriptions of their manias, depressions, and mixed states. Most of the rest of the accounts were from my patients or passages taken from the psychiatric literature. In a few instances, however, I used my own descriptions of my experiences that I had written for teaching purposes over the years. So interspersed throughout clinical studies, symptom frequencies, and classic clinical descriptions from the European and British medical literature were excerpts from poems, novels, and autobiographical accounts written by individuals who had suffered from manic-depressive illness.

Time and again, because of both personal and clinical experiences, I found myself emphasizing the terrible lethality of manic-depressive illness, the dreadful agitation involved in mixed manic states, and the importance of dealing with patients' reluctance to take lithium or other medications to control their moods. Having to stand back from my own feelings and past in order to write in a more cerebral, scholarly way was refreshing, and it forced me to structure and put into a more objective perspective the turmoil I had been through. Often, the science of the field was not only exciting, but it also held out the very realistic hope of new treatments. Although it was, on occasion, disturbing to see powerful and complicated emotions and behaviors distilled into deadeningly dull diagnostic phrases, it was hard not to be caught up in the new methods and findings of a very rapidly progressing field of clinical medicine.

I ended up strangely loving the discipline and obsessiveness that went into developing the countless tables of data. There was something lullingly reassuring about entering number after number, percentage after percentage, into the summary charts; critiquing the methods used in the various studies; and then trying to make some overall sense out of the large number of articles and books that had been reviewed. Much as I had done when frightened or upset as a child, I found that asking questions, tracking down answers as best I could, and then asking yet more questions was the best way to provide a distance from anxiety and a framework for understanding.

*L*owering my lithium level had allowed not only a clarity of thinking, but also a vividness and intensity of experience, back into my life; these elements had once formed the core of my normal temperament, and their absence had left gaping hollows in the way in which I could respond to the world. The too rigid structuring of my moods and temperament, which had resulted from a higher dose of lithium, made me less resilient to stress than a lower dose, which, like the building codes in California that are designed to prevent damage from earthquakes, allowed my mind and emotions to sway a bit. Therefore, and rather oddly, there was a new solidness to both my thinking and emotions. Gradually, as I began to look around me, I realized that this was the kind of evenness and predictability most people had, and probably took for granted, throughout their lives.

When I was an undergraduate I tutored a blind student in statistics; once a week he would make his way, with his guide dog, to my small office in the basement of the psychology building. I was very affected by working with him, seeing how difficult it was for him to do the things I so much took for granted and by watching the extraordinarily close relationship he had with his collie, who, having accompanied him to the office, would immediately curl up and fall asleep at his feet. As the term went on I felt increasingly comfortable in asking him about what it was like to be blind; what it was like to be blind, young, and an undergraduate at the University of California; and what it was like to have to be so dependent upon others to learn and survive. After several months I had deluded myself that I had at least some notion, however small, of what life was like for him. Then one day he asked me if I would mind meeting him for his tutorial session in the blind reading room of the undergraduate library, rather than in my office.

I tracked down the reading room with some difficulty and started to go in. I stopped suddenly when I realized with horror that the room was almost totally dark. It was dead silent, no lights were on, and yet there were half a dozen students bending over their books or listening intently to the audiotapes of the professors' lectures that they had recorded. A total chill went down my spine at the eeriness of the scene. My student heard me come in, got up, walked over to the light switch, and turned on the lights for me. It was one of those still, clear moments when you realize that you haven't understood anything at all, that you have had no real comprehension of the other person's world. As I gradually entered into the world of more stable moods and more predictable life, I began to realize that I knew very little about it and had no real idea of what it would be like to live in such a place. In many ways, I was a stranger to the normal world.

It was a sobering thought, and one that cut both ways. My moods still shifted often and precipitously enough to afford me occasional intoxicating, mind-on-the-edge experiences; these white manias were infused with the intense, high-flying exuberance, absolute assuredness of purpose, and easy cascading of ideas that had made taking lithium so difficult for so long. But then when the black tiredness inevitably followed, I would be subdued back into the recognition that I had a bad disease, one that could destroy all pleasure and hope and competence. I began to covet the day-to-day steadiness that most of my colleagues seemed to enjoy. I also began to appreciate how draining and preoccupying it had become just to keep my mind bobbing above water. It was true that much got done during the days and weeks of flying high, but it was also true that one generated new projects and made new commitments, which then had to be completed during the grayer times. I was constantly chasing the tail of my own brain, recovering from, or delving into, new moods and new experiences. The new was beginning to lack both newness and luster, and the mere accumulation of experiences was beginning to seem far less meaningful than I imagined exploring the depths of such experiences ought to be.

The extremes in my moods were not nearly as pronounced as they had been, but it was clear that a low-grade, fitful instability had become an integral part of my life. I had now, after many years, finally convinced myself that a certain intellectual steadiness was not only desirable, but essential; somewhere in my heart, however, I continued to believe that intense and lasting love was possible only in a climate of somewhat tumultuous passions. This, I felt, consigned me to being with a man whose temperament was largely similar to my own. I was late to understand that chaos and intensity are no substitute for lasting love, nor are they necessarily an improvement on real life. Normal people are not always boring. On the contrary. Volatility and passion, although often more romantic and enticing, are not intrinsically preferable to a steadiness of experience and feeling about another person (nor are they incompatible). These are beliefs, of course, that one has intuitively about friendships and family; they become less obvious when caught up in a romantic life that mirrors, magnifies, and perpetuates one's own mercurial emotional life and temperament. It has been with pleasure, and not-inconsiderable pain, that I have learned about the possibilities of love—its steadiness and its growth—from my husband, the man with whom I have lived for almost a decade.

I first met Richard Wyatt at a Christmas party in Washington, and he certainly was not at all what I expected. I had heard of him—he is a well-known schizophrenia researcher, Chief of Neuropsychiatry at the National Institute of Mental Health, and the author of more than seven hundred scientific papers and books—but I was completely unprepared for the handsome, unassuming, quietly charming man I found myself talking with near a gigantic Christmas tree. He was not only attractive, he was very easy to talk to, and we got together often in the months that followed. Less than a year after we met, I returned to London for another marvelous six months, again on sabbatical leave from UCLA, and then went back to Los Angeles long enough to fulfill my post-sabbatical obligations and make plans to move to Washington. The whole thing had been a short but very convincing courtship. I loved being with him and found him not just unbelievably smart, but imaginative, fiendishly curious, refreshingly open-minded, and wonderfully easygoing. Even then, very early in our relationship, I could not imagine my life without him. I resigned my tenured position at the medical school with genuine regret at leaving the University of California, which I loved, and considerable anxiety about the financial implications of giving up a secure income, and then went to a long round of farewell parties given by colleagues, friends, and students. Overall, however, I left Los Angeles with few regrets. It had never been the City of Angels to me, and I was more than happy to leave it, first, thousands of feet below me—and then, finally, thousands of miles behind—filled with near death, a completely shattered innocence, and a recurrently lost and broken mind. Life in California had been often good, even very wonderful, but it was hard for me to see any of that at the time I returned to Washington to live. The ever promising, always elusive, and infinitely complex Promised Land seemed to me to be exactly that: promised.

Richard and I moved into a house in Georgetown and quickly confirmed what our common sense should have told us: we could not have been more different. He was low-key, I was intense; things that cut me to the quick he was able to sail by with scarcely a notice; he was slow to anger, I quick; the world registered gently upon him, sometimes not at all, whereas I was fast to feel both pleasure and pain. He was, indeed, in most ways and at most times, a man of moderation; I was quicker to slight, quicker to sense, and perhaps quicker to reach out and attempt to heal hurts we inevitably caused one another. Concerts and opera, mainstays of my existence, were torture to him, as were long, extended talks or vacations lasting more than three days. We were a complete mismatch. I was filled with a thousand enthusiasms or black despair; Richard, who for the most part maintained an even emotional course, found it difficult to handle—or, worse yet, take seriously—my intensely mercurial moods. He had no idea what to do with me. If I asked him what he was thinking, it was never about death, the human condition, relationships, or us; it was, instead, almost always about a scientific problem or, occasionally, about a patient. He pursued his science and the practice of medicine with the same romantic intensity that was integral to the way I pursued the rest of life.

He was not, it was clear, going to gaze meaningfully into my eyes over long dinners and fine wines, nor discuss literature and music over late-night coffee and port. He, in fact, *couldn't* sit still very long, had a scarcely measurable attention span, didn't drink much, never touched coffee, and wasn't particularly interested in the complexities of relationships or the affirmations of art. He couldn't abide poetry and was genuinely amazed that I seemed to spend so much of my day just wandering around, rather aimlessly, going to the zoo, visiting art galleries, walking my dog—a sweet, wholly independent, morbidly shy basset hound named Pumpkin—or meeting friends for lunch and breakfast. Yet not once in the years we have been together have I doubted

Richard's love for me, nor mine for him. Love, like life, is much stranger and far more complicated than one is brought up to believe. Our common intellectual interests—medicine, science, and psychiatry—are very strong ones, and our differences in both substance and style have allowed each of us a great deal of independence, which has been essential and which, ultimately, has bound us very close to one another over the years. My life with Richard has become a safe harbor: an extremely interesting place, filled with love and warmth and always a bit open to the outer sea. But like all safe harbors that manage to retain fascination as well as safety, it was less than smooth sailing to reach.

When I first told Richard about my manic-depressive illness, soon after we met, he looked genuinely stunned. We were sitting in the main dining room of the Del Coronado Hotel in San Diego at the time; he slowly put down the hamburger he was eating, stared straight into my eyes, and, without missing a beat, said rather dryly, "That explains a lot." He was remarkably kind. Much as David Laurie had done, he asked me a great deal about what form my illness took and how it had affected my life. Perhaps because both were physicians, he, too, asked question after question of a more medical nature: what were my symptoms when I was manic, how depressed had I gotten, had I ever been suicidal, what medications had I taken in the past, what medications was I now taking, did I have any side effects. He was, as ever, low-key and reassuring; whatever deeper concerns he had, he was kind and smart enough to keep to himself.

But, as I well knew, an understanding at an abstract level does not necessarily translate into an understanding at a day-to-day level. I have become fundamentally and deeply skeptical that anyone who does not have this illness can truly understand it. And, ultimately, it is probably unreasonable to expect the kind of acceptance of it that one so desperately desires. It is not an illness that lends itself to easy empathy. Once a restless or frayed mood has turned to anger, or violence, or psychosis, Richard, like most, finds it very difficult to see it as illness, rather than as being willful, angry, irrational, or simply tiresome. What I experience as beyond my control can instead seem to him deliberate and frightening. It is, at these times, impossible for me to convey my desperation and pain; it is harder still, afterward, to recover from the damaging acts and dreadful words. These terrible black manias, with their agitated, ferocious, and savage sides, are understandably difficult for Richard to understand and almost as difficult for me to explain.

No amount of love can cure madness or unblacken one's dark moods. Love can help, it can make the pain more tolerable, but, always, one is beholden to medication that may or may not always work and may or may not be bearable. Madness, on the other hand, most certainly can, and often does, kill love through its mistrustfulness, unrelenting pessimism, discontents, erratic behavior, and, especially, through its savage moods. The sadder, sleepier, slower, and less volatile depressions are more intuitively understood and more easily taken in stride. A quiet melancholy is neither threatening nor beyond ordinary comprehension; an angry, violent, vexatious despair is both. Experience and love have, over much time, taught both of us a great deal about dealing with manic-depressive illness; I occasionally laugh and tell him that his imperturbability is worth three hundred milligrams of lithium a day to me, and it is probably true.

Sometimes, in the midst of one of my dreadful, destructive upheavals of mood, I feel Richard's quietness nearby and am reminded of Byron's wonderful description of the rainbow that sits "Like Hope upon a death-bed" on the verge of a wild, rushing cataract; yet, "while all around is torn / By the distracted waters," the rainbow stays serene:

> Resembling, 'mid the torture of the scene,
> Love watching Madness with unalterable mien.

But if love is not the cure, it certainly can act as a very strong medicine. As John Donne has written, it is not so pure and abstract as one might once have thought and wished, but it does endure, and it does grow.

Part Four

AN UNQUIET
MIND

Speaking of Madness

Not long before I left Los Angeles for Washington, I received the most vituperative and unpleasant letter that anyone has ever written me. It came not from a colleague or a patient, but from a woman who, having seen an announcement of a lecture I was to give, was outraged that I had used the word "madness" in the title of my talk. I was, she wrote, insensitive and crass and very clearly had no idea at all what it was like to suffer from something as awful as manic-depressive illness. I was just one more doctor who was climbing my way up the academic ranks by walking over the bodies of the mentally ill. I was shaken by the ferocity of the letter, resented it, but did end up thinking long and hard about the language of madness.

In the language that is used to discuss and describe mental illness, many different things—descriptiveness, banality, clinical precision, and stigma—intersect to create confusion, misunderstanding, and a gradual bleaching out of traditional words and phrases. It is no longer clear what place words such as "mad," "daft," "crazy," "cracked," or "certifiable" should have in a society increasingly sensitive to the feelings and rights of those who are mentally ill. Should, for example, expressive, often humorous, language—phrases such as "taking the fast trip to Squirrel City," being a "few apples short of a picnic," "off the wall," "around the bend," or "losing the bubble" (a British submariner's term for madness)—be held hostage to the fads and fashions of "correct" or "acceptable" language?

One of my friends, prior to being discharged from a psychiatric hospital after an acute manic episode, was forced to attend a kind of group therapy session designed as a consciousness-raising effort, one that encouraged the soon-to-be ex-patients not to use, or allow to be used in their presence, words such as "squirrel," "fruitcake," "nut," "wacko," "bat," or "loon." Using these words, it was felt, would "perpetuate a lack of self-esteem and self-stigmatization." My friend found the exercise patronizing and ridiculous. But was it? On the one hand, it was entirely laudable and professional, if rather excessively earnest, advice: the pain of hearing these words, in the wrong context or the wrong tone, is sharp; the memory of insensitivity and prejudice lasts for a long time. No doubt, too, allowing such language to go unchecked or uncorrected leads not only to personal pain, but contributes both directly and indirectly to discrimination in jobs, insurance, and society at large.

On the other hand, the assumption that rigidly rejecting words and phrases that have existed for centuries will have much impact on public attitudes is rather dubious. It gives an illusion of easy answers to impossibly difficult situations and ignores the powerful role of wit and irony as positive agents of self-notion and social change. Clearly there is a need for freedom, diversity, wit, and directness of language about abnormal mental states and behavior. Just as clearly, there is a profound need for a change in public perception about mental illness. The issue, of course, is one of context and emphasis. Science, for example, requires a highly precise language. Too frequently, the fears and misunderstandings of the public, the needs of science, the inanities of popularized psychology, and the goals of mental health advocacy get mixed together in a divisive confusion.

One of the best cases in point is the current confusion over the use of the increasingly popular term "bipolar disorder"—now firmly entrenched in the nomenclature of the *Diagnostic and Statistical Manual* (DSM-IV), the authoritative diagnostic system published by the American Psychiatric Association—instead of the historic term "manic-depressive illness." Although I always think of myself as a manic-depressive, my official DSM-IV diagnosis is "bipolar I disorder; recurrent; severe with psychotic features; full interepisode recovery" (one of the many DSM-IV diagnostic criteria I have "fulfilled" along the way, and a personal favorite, is an "excessive involvement in pleasurable activities"). Obviously, as a clinician and researcher, I strongly believe that scientific and clinical studies, in order to be pursued with accuracy and reliability, must be based on the kind of precise language and explicit diagnostic criteria that make up the core of DSM-IV. No patient or family member is well served by elegant and expressive language if it is also imprecise and subjective. As a person and patient, however, I find the word "bipolar" strangely and powerfully offensive: it seems to me to obscure and minimize the illness it is supposed to represent. The description "manic-depressive," on the other hand, seems to capture both the nature and the seriousness of the disease I have, rather than attempting to paper over the reality of the condition.

Most clinicians and many patients feel that "bipolar disorder" is less stigmatizing than "manic-depressive illness." Perhaps so, but perhaps not. Certainly, patients who have suffered from the illness should have the right to choose whichever term they feel more comfortable with. But two questions arise: Is the term "bipolar" really a medically accurate one, and does changing the name of a condition actually lead to a greater acceptance of it? The answer to the first question, which concerns accuracy, is that "bipolar" is accurate in the sense that it indicates an individual has suffered from both mania (or mild forms of mania) and depression, unlike those individuals who have suffered from depression alone. But splitting mood disorders into bipolar and unipolar categories presupposes a distinction between depression and manic-depressive illness—both clinically and etiologically—that is not always clear, nor supported by science. Likewise, it perpetuates the notion that depression exists rather tidily segregated on its own pole, while mania clusters off neatly and discreetly on another. This polarization of two clinical states flies in the face of everything that we know about the cauldronous, fluctuating nature of manic-depressive illness; it ignores the question of whether mania is, ultimately, simply an extreme form of depression; and it minimizes the importance of mixed manic-and-depressive states, conditions that are common, extremely important clinically, and lie at the heart of many of the critical theoretical issues underlying this particular disease.

But the question also arises whether, ultimately, the destigmatization of mental illness comes about from merely a change in the language or, instead, from aggressive public education efforts; from successful treatments, such as lithium, the anticonvulsants, antidepressants, and antipsychotics; from treatments that are not only successful, but somehow also catch the imagination of the public and media (Prozac's influence on public opinion and knowledge about depression, for example); from discovery of the underlying genetic or other biological causes of mental illness; from brain-imaging techniques, such as PET and MRI (magnetic resonance imaging) scans, that visually communicate the location and concrete existence of these disorders; from the development of blood tests that will ultimately give medical credibility to psychiatric diseases; or from legislative actions, such as the Americans with Disabilities Act, and the obtainment of parity with other medical conditions under whatever health-reform system is put into place. Attitudes about mental illness are changing, however glacially, and it is in large measure due to a combination of these things—successful treatment, advocacy, and legislation.

The major mental health advocacy groups are made up primarily of patients, family members, and mental health professionals. They have been particularly effective in educating the public, the media, and the state and national governments. Although very different in styles and goals, these groups have provided direct support for tens of thousands of individual patients and their families; have raised the level of medical care in their communities by insisting upon competence and respect through, in effect, boycotting those psychiatrists and psychologists who do not provide both; and have agitated, badgered, and cajoled members of Congress (many of whom themselves suffer from mood disorders or have mental illness in their families) into increasing money for research, proposing parity for psychiatric illnesses, and passing legislation that bans job and insurance discrimination against the mentally ill. These groups—and the scientists and clinicians who make treatment possible—have made life easier for all of us who have psychiatric illnesses, whether we call ourselves mad or write letters of protest to those who do. Because of them, we now have the luxury of being able to debate the fine points of language about our own and the human condition.

The Troubled Helix

Seated in a chair, with quick
access to escape through the back door of the conference room, Jim Watson was twitching, peering,
scanning, squinting, and yawning. His fingers, linked
together on the top of his head, were tapping restlessly,
and he alternately was paying avid, if fleeting, attention
to the data being presented, snatching a look at his *New
York Times*, and drifting off into his own version of
planetary wanderings. Jim is not good at looking interested when he is bored, and it was impossible to know
if he really was thinking about the science at hand—the
genetics and molecular biology of manic-depressive
illness—or was instead mulling about politics, gossip,
love, potential financial donors for Cold Spring Harbor Laboratory, architecture, tennis, or whatever other
heated and passionate enthusiasm occupied his mind
and heart at the moment. An intense and exceedingly
blunt man, he is not someone who tends to bring out
the dispassionate side of people. For myself, I find him
fascinating and very wonderful. Jim is genuinely

independent and, in an increasingly bland world, a true zebra among horses. While it could be argued that it is relatively easy to be independent and unpredictable if you have won the Nobel Prize for your contributions to discovering the structure of life, it is also clear that the same underlying temperament—intense, competitive, imaginative, and iconoclastic—helped propel his initial pursuit for the structure of DNA.

Jim's palpably high energy level is also very appealing; his pace, whether intellectual or physical, can be exhausting, and trying to keep up with him, in discussions across the dinner table or walking the grounds of Cold Spring Harbor, is no mean task. His wife maintains she can tell whether or not Jim is in the house simply by the amount of energy she feels in the air. But however interesting he is as a person, Jim is first and foremost a scientific leader: director until only very recently of one of the foremost molecular biology laboratories in the world, Cold Spring Harbor Laboratory, and the first director of the National Center for Human Genome Research. In the past few years, he has turned his interest toward the search for the genes responsible for manic-depressive illness.

Because the scientific understanding of manic-depressive illness is so ultimately beholden to the field of molecular biology, it is a world in which I have spent an increasing amount of time. It is an exotic world, one developed around an odd assortment of plants and animals—maize, fruit flies, yeast, worms, mice, humans, puffer fish—and it contains a somewhat strange, rapidly evolving, and occasionally quite poetic language system filled with marvelous terms like "orphan clones," "plasmids," and "high-density cosmids"; "triple helices," "untethered DNA," and "kamikaze reagents", "chromosome walking," "gene hunters," and "gene mappers." It is a field clearly in pursuit of the most fundamental of understandings, a search for the biological equivalent of quarks and leptons.

The meeting where Watson was peering and twitching and yawning was focused specifically on the genetic basis of manic-depressive illness, with the intent of bringing together clinical psychiatrists, geneticists, and molecular biologists, all of whom are in one way or another actively engaged in the search for the genes responsible for manic-depressive illness, to share information about their research methods, findings, and the pedigrees of the affected families whose genetic material is being analyzed. Pedigree after pedigree was being projected onto the screen, some with relatively few ill family members, others containing large numbers of squares and circles that had been completely blackened in, indicating men or women who suffered from manic-depressive illness. Half-blackened circles and squares depicted depressive illness, and an *s,* cross, or slash flagged those individuals who had committed suicide. Each of these black or half-black symbols represented a life with periods of terrible suffering, yet, ironically, the more of these darkened squares and circles in a particular family, the "better" (that is, the more genetically informative and useful) the pedigree was considered to be. It seemed very likely, when I looked around the room, that among these scientists, and somewhere within these pedigrees, the location of the gene or genes responsible for manic-depressive illness was going to be found. It was a very exciting thought, because once the genes are located, early and far more accurate diagnosis is likely to follow; so, too, is more specific, safer, less problematic, and more effective treatment.

The slides went off, the curtains were pulled back, and I looked out beyond Jim Watson, past the apple trees, and remembered a trip I had taken, years ago, down the Mississippi. Mogens Schou, a Danish psychiatrist who, more than anyone, is responsible for the introduction of lithium as a treatment for manic-depressive illness, and I had decided to skip a day's sessions of the American Psychiatric Association's annual meeting and take advantage of being in New Orleans. The best way to do this, we decided, was to take a boat ride down the Mississippi River. It was a gorgeous day, and, after having discussed a wide variety of topics, Mogens turned to me and asked me point-blank, Why are you *really* studying mood disorders? I must have looked as taken aback and uncomfortable as I felt, because, changing tack, he said, "Well, why don't I tell you why *I* study mood disorders?" He proceeded to tell me about all of the depression and manic-depressive illness in his family, how devastating it had been, and how, because of this, years ago, he had been desperately searching the medical literature for any new, experimental treatments. When John Cade's article about the use of lithium in acute mania first appeared in 1949, in an obscure Australian medical journal, Mogens pounced on it and began almost immediately the rigorous clinical trials necessary to establish the efficacy and safety of the drug. He talked with ease about his family history of mental illness and emphasized that it had been this strongly personal motivation that had driven virtually all of his research. He made it clear to me that he suspected my involvement in clinical research about manic-depressive illness was likewise personally motivated.

Feeling a bit trapped, but also relieved, I decided to be honest about my own and my family's history, and soon the two of us were drawing our pedigrees on the backs of table napkins. I was amazed at how many of my squares and circles were darkened, or darkened with a question mark placed underneath (I knew, for instance, that my great-uncle had spent virtually all of his adult life in an asylum, but I didn't know what his diagnosis had been). Manic-depressive illness occurred repeatedly, throughout the three generations I had knowledge of, on my father's side of the family; asterisks, representing suicide attempts, showed up like a starfield. My mother's side of the family, in comparison, was squeaky clean. It would not have taken a very astute observer of human nature to figure out that my parents are terribly different, but here was one very concrete example of their differences—and, quite literally, in black and white. Mogens, who had been sketching out his own family tree, took one look over my shoulder at the number of affected members in mine and promptly, laughingly, conceded the "battle of the black boxes." He noted that the circle representing me was solid black and had an asterisk next to it—how remarkable to be able to reduce one's suicide attempt to a simple symbol!—so we talked for a long time about my illness, lithium, its side effects, and my suicide attempt.

Talking with Mogens was extremely helpful, in part because he aggressively encouraged me to use my own experiences in my research, writing, and teaching, and in part because it was very important to me to be able to talk with a senior professor who not only had some knowledge of what I had been through, but who had used his own experiences to make a profound difference in the lives of hundreds of thousands of people. Including my own. No matter what struggles I had had with lithium, it was painfully clear to me that without it I would have been long dead or on the back wards of a state hospital. I was one of many who owed their lives to the black circles and squares in Schou's family tree.

The fact that manic-depressive illness is a genetic disease brings with it, not surprisingly, very complicated and often difficult emotions. At one extreme is the terrible shame and guilt one can be made to feel. Many years ago, when I was living in Los Angeles, I went to a physician recommended to me by a colleague. After examining me, and after finding out that I had been on lithium for many years, he asked me an extended series of questions about my psychiatric history. He also asked me whether or not I planned to have children. Having generally been treated with intelligence and compassion by my various doctors up to that point, I had no reason to be anything but direct about my extensive history of mania and depression, although I also made it clear that I was, in the vernacular, a "good lithium responder." I told him that I very much wanted to have children, which immediately led to his asking me what I planned to do about taking lithium during pregnancy. I started to tell him that it seemed obvious to me that the dangers of my illness far outweighed any potential problems that lithium might cause a developing fetus, and that I therefore would choose to stay on lithium. Before I finished, however, he broke in to ask me if I knew that manic-depressive illness was a genetic disease. Stifling for the moment an urge to remind him that I had spent my entire professional life studying manic-depressive illness and that, in any event, I wasn't entirely stupid, I said, "Yes, of course." At that point, in an icy and imperious voice that I can hear to this day, he stated—as though it were God's truth, which he no doubt felt that it was—"You shouldn't have children. You have manic-depressive illness."

I felt sick, unbelievably and utterly sick, and deeply humiliated. Determined to resist being provoked into what would, without question, be interpreted as irrational behavior, I asked him if his concerns about my having children stemmed from the fact that, because of my illness, he thought I would be an inadequate mother or simply that he thought it was best to avoid bringing another manic-depressive into the world. Ignoring or missing my sarcasm, he replied, "Both." I asked him to leave the room, put on the rest of my clothes, knocked on his office door, told him to go to hell, and left. I walked across the street to my car, sat down, shaking, and sobbed until I was exhausted. Brutality takes many forms, and what he had done was not only brutal but unprofessional and uninformed. It did the kind of lasting damage that only something that cuts so quick and deep to the heart can do.

Oddly enough, it had never occurred to me not to have children simply because I had manic-depressive illness. Even in my blackest depressions, I never regretted having been born. It is true that I had wanted to die, but that is peculiarly different from regretting having been born. Overwhelmingly, I was enormously glad to have been born, grateful for life, and I couldn't imagine not wanting to pass on life to someone else. All things considered, I had had a marvelous—albeit turbulent and occasionally awful—existence. Of course, I had had serious concerns: How could one not? Would I, for example, be able to take care of my children properly? What would happen to them if I got severely depressed? Much more frightening still, what would happen to them if I got manic, if my judgment became impaired, if I became violent or uncontrollable? How would it be to have to watch my own children struggle with depression, hopelessness, despair, or insanity if they themselves became ill? Would I watch them too hawkishly for symptoms or mistake their normal reactions to life as signs of illness? All of these were things I had thought about a thousand times, but never, not once, had I questioned *having* children. And despite the cold-bloodedness of the doctor who examined me and who told me I shouldn't, I would have delighted in having a houseful of children, as David and I once had planned. But it just didn't work out that way: David died, and Richard—the only man since David's death that I wanted to have children with—already had three from a previous marriage.

Not having children of my own is the single most intolerable regret of my life. I do, however, and very fortunately, have two nephews and a niece—each wonderful and quite remarkable in his or her own way—and I enjoy, beyond description, my relationships with them. Being an aunt is an extraordinarily pleasurable sort of thing, especially if your nephews and niece are reflective, independent, thoughtful, droll, smart, and imaginative people. It is impossible not to find their company delightful. My nephews, whose interests, like those of their father, have leaned toward the study of mathematics and economics, are quiet, witty, freethinking, gentle souled, and charming young men. My niece, considerably younger, is now eleven and, having already won a national writing award, is very determined to become a writer. One often finds her curled up in a chair, scribbling away, asking about words or people, tending to her many and various animals, or leaping mouth first into a family discussion to defend her point of view. She is fiery, sensitive, original, and disconcertingly able to hold her own against a very vociferously articulate pack of older brothers, parents, and sundry other adults. I cannot imagine the awful gap that would exist in my life without these three children.

*N*ow and again, despite my strong commitment to the scientific efforts that are being made to track down the genes for manic-depressive illness, I have concerns about what finding the genes might actually mean. Clearly, if better and earlier diagnosis and more specific, less troublesome treatments result from the ongoing genetic research, then the benefits to individuals who have manic-depressive illness, to their families, and to society will be extraordinary. It is, in fact, only a matter of time until these benefits will be available. But what are the dangers in prenatal diagnostic testing? Will prospective parents choose to abort fetuses that carry the genes for manic-depressive illness, even though it is a treatable disease? (Interestingly, a recent study done at Johns Hopkins, which asked manic-depressive patients and their spouses whether or not they would abort an affected fetus, found that very few said that they would.) Do we risk making the world a blander, more homogenized place if we get rid of the genes for manic-depressive ill-ness—an admittedly impossibly complicated scientific problem? What are the risks to the risk takers, those restless individuals who join with others in society to propel the arts, business, politics, and science? Are manic-depressives, like spotted owls and clouded leop-ards, in danger of becoming an "endangered species"?

These are very difficult ethical issues, particularly because manic-depressive illness can confer advantages on both the individual and society. The disease, in both its severe and less severe forms, appears to convey its advantages not only through its relationship to the artis-tic temperament and imagination, but through its influ-ence on many eminent scientists, as well as business, religious, military, and political leaders. Subtler effects—such as those on personality, thinking style, and energy—are also involved because it is a common ill-ness with a wide range of temperamental, behavioral, and cognitive expression. The situation is yet further complicated by the fact that additional genetic, bio-chemical, and environmental factors (such as exposure to prolonged or significant changes in light, pro-nounced sleep reduction, childbirth, drug or alcohol use) may be at least in part responsible for both the ill-ness and the cognitive and temperamental characteris-tics associated with great achievement. These scientific and ethical issues are real ones; fortunately, they are being actively considered by the federal government's Genome Project and other groups of scientists and ethicists. But they are immensely troubling problems and will remain so for many years to come.

Science remains quite remarkable in its ability to raise new problems even as it solves old ones. It moves quickly, often beautifully, and as it moves it brings high expectations in its wake.

Sitting on one of the hard, uncomfortable chairs that are so characteristic of medical conferences, I was semi-oblivious to the world. My mind was on hold after having been lulled into a mild hypnotic state by the click, click, click of the changing of slides in a carousel. My eyes were open, but my brain was swaying gently in its hammock, tucked away in the far back reaches of my skull. It was dark and stuffy in the room, but beautiful and snowing outside. A group of my colleagues and I were in the Colorado Rockies, and anyone with any sense at all was skiing; yet there were more than a hundred doctors in the room, and the slides were going click, click, click. I caught myself thinking, for the hundredth time, that being crazy doesn't necessarily mean being stupid, and what on earth was I doing indoors instead of being out on the slopes? Suddenly, my ears perked up. A flat, numbingly objective voice was mumbling something about giving an "update on structural brain abnormalities in bipolar illness." My structurally abnormal brain came to attention, and a chill shot down my spine. The mumbling continued: "In the bipolar patients we have studied, there is a significantly increased number of small areas of focal signal hyperintensities [areas of increased water concentration] suggestive of abnormal tissue. These are what neurologists sometimes refer to as 'unidentified bright objects,' or UBOs."The audience laughed appreciatively.

I, who could ill afford any more loss of brain tissue—God knows what little chunks of gray matter had crossed the River Styx after my nearly lethal lithium overdose—laughed with somewhat less than total enthusiasm. The speaker went on, "The medical significance of these UBOs is unclear, but we know that they are associated with other conditions, such as Alzheimer's, multiple sclerosis, and multi-infarct dementias." I was right; I should have gone skiing. Against my better judgment, I pointed my head in the direction of the screen. The slides were riveting, and, as always, I was captivated by the unbelievable detail of the structure of the brain that was revealed by the newest versions of MRI techniques. There is a beauty and an intuitive appeal to the brain-scanning methods, especially the high-resolution MRI pictures and the gorgeous multicolored scans from the PET studies. With PET, for example, a depressed brain will show up in cold, brain-inactive deep blues, dark purples, and hunter greens; the same brain when hypomanic, however, is lit up like a Christmas tree, with vivid patches of bright reds and yellows and oranges. Never has the color and structure of science so completely captured the cold inward deadness of depression or the vibrant, active engagement of mania.

There is a wonderful kind of excitement in modern neuroscience, a romantic, moon-walk sense of exploring and setting out for new frontiers. The science is elegant, the scientists dismayingly young, and the pace of discovery absolutely staggering. Like the molecular biologists, the brain-scanners are generally well aware of the extraordinary frontiers they are crossing, and it would take a mind that is on empty, or a heart made of stone, to be unmoved by their collective ventures and enthusiasms.

I was, in spite of myself, caught up by the science, wondering whether these hyperintensities were the cause or the effect of illness, whether they became more pronounced over time, where in the brain they localized, whether they were related to the problems in spatial orientation and facial recognition that I and many other manic-depressives experience, and whether children who were at risk for manic-depressive illness, because one or both of their parents had the disease, would show these brain abnormalities even before they became ill. The clinical side of my mind began to mull about the visual advantages of these and other imaging findings in convincing some of my more literary and skeptical patients that (a) there *is* a brain, (b) their moods are related to their brains, and (c) there may be specific brain-damaging effects of going off their medications. These speculations kept me distracted for a while, as changing gears from the personal side of having manic-depressive illness to the professional role of studying and treating it often does. But, invariably, the personal interest and concerns returned.

When I got back to Johns Hopkins, where I was now teaching, I buttonholed neurology colleagues and grilled my associates who were doing the MRI studies. I scurried off to the library to read up on what was known; it is, after all, one thing to believe intellectually that this disease is in your brain; it is quite another thing to actually see it. Even the titles of some of the articles were a bit ungluing: "Basal Ganglia Volumes and White Matter Hyperintensities in Patients with Bipolar Disorder," "Structural Brain Abnormalities in Bipolar Affective Disorder: Ventricular Enlargement and Focal Signal Hyperintensities," "Subcortical Abnormalities Detected in Bipolar Affective Disorders, Using Magnetic Resonance Imaging"; on and on they went. I sat down to read. One study found that "Of the 32 scans of the patients with bipolar disorder, 11 (34.4%) showed hyperintensities, while only one scan (3.2%) from the normal comparison group contained such abnormalities."

After an inward snort about "normal comparison group," I read on and found that, as usual in new fields of clinical medicine, there were far more questions than answers, and it was unclear what any of these findings really meant: they could be due to problems in measurement, they could be explained by dietary or treatment history, they could be due to something totally unrelated to manic-depressive illness; there could be any number of other explanations. The odds were very strong, however, that the UBOs meant *something*. In a strange way, though, after reading through a long series of studies, I ended up more reassured and less frightened. The very fact that the science was moving so quickly had a way of generating hope, and, if the changes in the brain structure did turn out to be meaningful, I was glad that first-class researchers were studying them. Without science, there would be no such hope. No hope at all.

And, whatever else, it certainly gave new meaning to the concept of losing one's mind.

Clinical Privileges

There is no easy way to tell other people that you have manic-depressive illness; if there is, I haven't found it. So despite the fact that most people that I have told have been very understanding—some remarkably so—I remain haunted by those occasions when the response was unkind, condescending, or lacking in even a semblance of empathy. The thought of discussing my illness in a more public forum has been, until quite recently, almost inconceivable. Much of this reluctance has been for professional reasons, but some has resulted from the cruelty, intentional or otherwise, that I have now and again experienced from colleagues or friends that I have chosen to confide in. It is what I have come to think of, not without bitterness, as the Mouseheart factor.

Mouseheart, a former colleague of mine in Los Angeles, was also, I thought, a friend. A soft-spoken psychoanalyst, he was someone I was in the habit of getting together with for a morning coffee. Less frequently, but enjoyably, we would go out for a long lunch and talk about our work and our lives. After some time, I began to feel the usual discomfort I tend to experience whenever a certain level of friendship or intimacy has been reached in a relationship and I have not mentioned my illness. It is, after all, not just an illness, but something that affects every aspect of my life: my moods, my temperament, my work, and my reactions to almost everything that comes my way. Not talking about manic-depressive illness, if only to discuss it once, generally consigns a friendship to a certain inevitable level of superficiality. With an inward sigh, I decided to go ahead and tell him.

We were in an oceanfront restaurant in Malibu at the time, so—after a brief rundown on my manias, depressions, and suicide attempt—I fixed my eye on a distant pile of rocks out in the ocean and waited for his response. It was a long, cold wait. Finally, I saw tears running down his face, and, although I remember thinking at the time that it was an extreme response— particularly since I had tried to present my manias in as lighthearted a way as possible, and my depressions with some dispassion—I thought it was touching that he felt so strongly about what I had been through. Then Mouseheart, wiping away his tears, told me that he just couldn't believe it. He was, he said, "deeply disappointed." He had thought I was so wonderful, so strong: How *could* I have attempted suicide? What had I been thinking? It was such an act of cowardice, so selfish.

I realized, to my horror, that he was serious. I was absolutely transfixed. His pain at hearing that I had manic-depressive illness was, it would seem, far worse than mine at actually having it. For a few minutes, I felt like Typhoid Mary. Then I felt betrayed, deeply embarrassed, and utterly exposed. His solicitude, of course, knew no bounds. Had I *really* been psychotic? If so, he asked in his soft voice, with seemingly infinite concern, did I really think, under the circumstances, that I was going to be able to handle the stresses of academic life? I pointed out to him, through clenched teeth, that I had in fact handled those particular stresses for many years, and, indeed, if truth be told, I was considerably younger than he was and had, in fact, published considerably more. I don't really remember much of the rest of the lunch, except that it was an ordeal, and that at some point, with sarcasm that managed to pass him by, I told him that he ought not to worry, that manic-depressive illness wasn't contagious (although he could have benefited from a bit of mania, given his rather dreary, obsessive, and humorless view of the world). He squirmed in his seat and averted his eyes.

A boxed bouquet of a dozen long-stemmed red roses arrived at my clinic the next morning; an abject note of apology was tucked in at the top. It was a nice thought, I suppose, but it didn't begin to salve the wound inflicted by what I knew had been a candid response on his part: he was normal, I was not, and—in those most killing of words—he was "deeply disappointed."

*T*here are many reasons why I have been reluctant to be open about having manic-depressive illness; some of the reasons are personal, many are professional. The personal issues revolve, to a large extent, around issues of family privacy—especially because the illness under consideration is a genetic one—as well as a general belief that personal matters should be kept personal. Too, I have been very concerned, perhaps unduly so, with how knowing that I have manic-depressive illness will affect people's perception of who I am and what I do. There is a thin line between what is considered zany and what is thought to be—a ghastly but damning word—"inappropriate," and only a sliverish gap exists between being thought intense, or a bit volatile, and being dismissively labeled "unstable." And, for whatever reasons of personal vanity, I dread the fact that my suicide attempt and depressions will be seen by some as acts of weakness or as "neurotic." Somehow, I don't mind the thought of being seen as intermittently psychotic nearly as much as I mind being pigeonholed as weak and neurotic. Finally, I am deeply wary that by speaking publicly or writing about such intensely private aspects of my life, I will return to them one day and find them bleached of meaning and feeling. By putting myself in the position of speaking too freely and too often, I am concerned that the experiences will become remote, inaccessible, and far distant, behind me; I fear that the experiences will become those of someone else rather than my own.

My major concerns about discussing my illness, however, have tended to be professional in nature. Early in my career, these concerns were centered on fears that the California Board of Medical Examiners would not grant me a license if it knew about my manic-depression. As time went by, I became less afraid of such administrative actions—primarily because I had worked out such an elaborate system of clinical safeguards, had told my close colleagues, and had discussed ad nauseam with my psychiatrist every conceivable contingency and how best to mitigate it—but I became increasingly concerned that my professional anonymity in teaching and research, such as it was, would be compromised. At UCLA, for example, I lectured and supervised large numbers of psychiatric residents and psychology interns in the clinic I directed; at Johns Hopkins I teach residents and medical students on the inpatient wards and in the outpatient mood disorders clinic. I cringe at the thought that these residents and interns may, in deference to what they perceive to be my feelings, not say what they really think or not ask the questions that they otherwise should and would ask.

Many of these concerns carry over into my research and writing. I have written extensively in medical and scientific journals about manic-depressive illness. Will my work now be seen by my colleagues as somehow biased because of my illness? It is a discomforting thought, although one of the advantages of science is that one's work, ultimately, is either replicated or it is not. Biases, because of this, tend to be minimized over time. I worry, however, about my colleagues' reactions once I am open about my illness: if, for example, I am attending a scientific meeting and ask a question, or challenge a speaker, will my question be treated as though it is coming from someone who has studied and treated mood disorders for many years, or will it instead be seen as a highly subjective, idiosyncratic view of someone who has a personal ax to grind? It is an awful prospect, giving up one's cloak of academic objectivity. But, of course, my work *has* been tremendously colored by my emotions and my experiences. They have deeply affected my teaching, my advocacy work, my clinical practice, and what I have chosen to study: manic-depressive illness in general and, more specifically, suicide, psychosis, psychological aspects of the disease and its treatment, lithium noncompliance, positive features of mania and cyclothymia, and the importance of psychotherapy.

Most important, however, as a clinician, I have had to consider the question that Mouseheart so artfully managed to slip into our lunchtime conversation in Malibu: Do I *really* think that someone with mental illness should be allowed to treat patients?

*W*hen I left the University of California in the winter of 1986 to return to Washington, I was eager to continue teaching and to obtain an academic appointment at a university medical school. Richard, who had gone to medical school at Johns Hopkins, thought I would love it. At his suggestion, I applied to the Department of Psychiatry for a faculty appointment, and I started teaching at Hopkins within a few months of moving back East. Richard was right. I loved Hopkins straightaway. And, as he predicted, one of the many pleasures I found in being on the Hopkins faculty was the seriousness with which teaching obligations are taken. The excellence of clinical care was another. It was only a matter of time. The issue of clinical privileges was bound to come up.

With the usual sense of profound uneasiness that for me accompanies having to look through official hospital appointment forms, I stared at the packet of papers in front of me. In imposing capital letters THE JOHNS HOPKINS HOSPITAL was written across the top of the page. Scanning downward, I saw that it was, as I had expected, an application for clinical privileges. Hoping for the best, but expecting the worst, I decided to tackle all of the straightforward questions first; I quickly checked "no" to a long series of questions about professional liability, malpractice insurance, and professional sanctions: During the previous application period, had I been involved in any litigation involving malpractice or professional liability? Were there any restrictions or limitations in my malpractice coverage? Had my license to practice ever been limited, suspended, subject to any conditions, terms of probation, formal or informal reprimand, not renewed, or revoked? Had I ever been subject to disciplinary action in any medical organization? Were there any disciplinary actions pending against me?

These questions, thank God, were easy to answer, having managed thus far, in a ridiculously litigious age, to avoid being sued for malpractice. It was the next section, "Personal Information," that made my heart race; and, sure enough, before too long I found the question that was going to require something more than just a checkmark in the "no" column:

> *Are you currently suffering from, or receiving treatment for any disability or illness, including drug or alcohol abuse, that would impair the proper performance of your duties and responsibilities at this hospital?*

Five lines down was the hangman's clause:

> *I fully understand that any significant misstatements in, or omissions from, this application may constitute cause for denial of appointment to or summary dismissal from the medical staff.*

I read back over the "Are you currently suffering from" question, thought about it for a long time, and finally wrote next to it "Per discussion with the chairman of the Department of Psychiatry." Then with a sinking feeling in my stomach, I telephoned my chairman at Hopkins and asked him if we could get together for lunch.

A week or so later, we met at the hospital restaurant. He was as talkative and funny as ever, so we spent several pleasant minutes catching up on departmental activities, teaching, research grants, and psychiatric politics. With my hands clenched in my lap and my heart in my throat, I told him about the clinical privileges form, my manic-depressive illness, and the treatment I was receiving for it. My closest colleague at Hopkins already knew about my illness, as I had always told those physicians with whom I most closely practiced. At UCLA, for example, I had discussed my illness in detail with the physicians who, with me, had set up the UCLA Affective Disorders Clinic and then, subsequently, with the doctor who had been the medical director of the clinic during virtually all of the years I was its director. My chairman at UCLA also knew that I was being treated for manic-depressive illness. I felt then, as I do now, that there should be safeguards in place in the event that my clinical judgment became impaired due to mania or severe depression. If I did not tell them, not only would the care of patients be jeopardized, but I would be placing my colleagues in an untenable position of professional and legal risk as well.

I made it clear to each of the doctors I worked closely with that I was under the care of an excellent psychiatrist, taking medication, and had no alcohol or drug abuse problem. I also asked them to feel free to ask my psychiatrist whatever questions they felt they needed to about my illness and my competence to practice (my psychiatrist, in turn, was asked to communicate both to me, and to whomever else he thought necessary, if he had any concerns about my clinical judgment). My colleagues agreed that if they had any doubts whatsoever about my clinical judgment they would tell me directly, immediately remove me from any patient care responsibilities, and alert my psychiatrist. I think that all of them have, at one time or another, spoken with my psychiatrist in order to obtain information about my illness and treatment; fortunately, none have ever had to contact him because of concerns about my clinical performance. Nor have I ever had to give up my clinical privileges, although I have, on my own, canceled or rescheduled appointments when I felt it would be in the best interests of patients.

I have been both fortunate and careful. The possibility always exists that my illness, or the illness of any clinician, for that matter, might interfere with clinical judgment. Questions about hospital privileges are neither unfair nor irrelevant. I don't like having to answer them, but they are completely reasonable. The privilege to practice is exactly that, a privilege; it is not a right. The real dangers, of course, come about from those clinicians (or, indeed, from those politicians, pilots, businessmen, or other individuals responsible for the welfare and lives of others) who—because of the stigma or the fear of suspension of their privileges or expulsion from medical school, graduate school, or residency— are hesitant to seek out psychiatric treatment. Left untreated, or unsupervised, many become ill, endangering not only their own lives but the lives of others; often, in an attempt to medicate their own moods, many doctors will also become alcoholics or drug abusers. It is not uncommon for depressed physicians to prescribe antidepressant medications for themselves; the results can be disastrous.

Hospitals and professional organizations need to acknowledge the extent to which untreated doctors, nurses, and psychologists present risks to the patients they treat. But they also need to encourage effective and compassionate treatment and work out guidelines for safeguards and intelligent, nonpaternalistic supervision. Untreated mood disorders result in risks not only to patients, but to the doctors themselves. Far too many doctors—many of them excellent physicians—commit suicide each year; one recent study concluded that, until quite recently, the United States lost annually the equivalent of a medium-sized medical school class from suicide alone. Most physician suicides are due to depression or manic-depressive illness, both of which are eminently treatable. Physicians, unfortunately, not only suffer from a higher rate of mood disorders than the general population, they also have a greater access to very effective means of suicide.

Doctors, of course, need first to heal themselves; but they also need accessible, competent treatment that allows them to heal. The medical and administrative system that harbors them must be one that encourages treatment, provides reasonable guidelines for supervised practice, but also one that does not tolerate incompetence or jeopardize patient care. Doctors, as my chairman is fond of pointing out, are there to treat patients; patients never should have to pay—either literally or medically—for the problems and sufferings of their doctors. I strongly agree with him about this; so it was not without a sense of dread that I waited for his response to my telling him that I was being treated for manic-depressive illness, and that I needed to discuss the issue of my hospital privileges with him. I watched his face for some indication of how he felt. Suddenly, he reached across the table, put his hand on mine, and smiled. "Kay, dear," he said, "I *know* you have manic-depressive illness." He paused, and then laughed. "If we got rid of all of the manic-depressives on the medical school faculty, not only would we have a much smaller faculty, it would also be a far more boring one."

A Life in Moods

We are all, as Byron put it, differently organized. We each move within the restraints of our temperament and live up only partially to its possibilities. Thirty years of living with manic-depressive illness has made me increasingly aware of both the restraints and possibilities that come with it. The ominous, dark, and deathful quality that I felt as a young child watching the high clear skies fill with smoke and flames *is* always there, somehow laced into the beauty and vitality of life. That darkness is an integral part of who I am, and it takes no effort of imagination on my part to remember the months of relentless blackness and exhaustion, or the terrible efforts it took in order to teach, read, write, see patients, and keep relationships alive. More deeply layered over but all too readily summoned up with the first trace of depression are the unforgettable images of violence, utter madness, mortifying behavior, and moods savage to experience, and even more disturbingly brutal in their effects upon others.

Yet however genuinely dreadful these moods and memories have been, they have always been offset by the elation and vitality of others; and whenever a mild and gentlish wave of brilliant and bubbling manic enthusiasm comes over me, I am transported by its exuberance—as surely as one is transported by a pungent scent into a world of profound recollection—to earlier, more intense and passionate times. The vividness that mania infuses into one's experiences of life creates strong, keenly recollected states, much as war must, and love and early memories surely do. Because of this, there is now, for me, a rather bittersweet exchange of a comfortable and settled present existence for a troubled but intensely lived past.

There are still occasional sirens to this past, and there remains a seductive, if increasingly rare, desire to recreate the furor and fever of earlier times. I look back over my shoulder and feel the presence of an intense young girl and then a volatile and disturbed young woman, both with high dreams and restless, romantic aspirations: How could one, should one, recapture that intensity or reexperience the glorious moods of dancing all night and into the morning, the gliding through starfields and dancing along the rings of Saturn, the zany manic enthusiasms? How can one ever bring back the long summer days of passion, the remembrance of lilacs, ecstasy, and gin fizzes that spilled down over a garden wall, and the peals of riotous laughter that lasted until the sun came up or the police arrived?

There is, for me, a mixture of longings for an earlier age; this is inevitable, perhaps, in any life, but there is an extra twist of almost painful nostalgia brought about by having lived a life particularly intense in moods. This makes it even harder to leave the past behind, and life, on occasion, becomes a kind of elegy for lost moods. I miss the lost intensities, and I find myself unconsciously reaching out for them, as I still now and again reach back with my hand for the fall and heaviness of my now-gone, long, thick hair; like the trace of moods, only a phantom weight remains. These current longings are, for the most part, only longings, and I do not feel compelled to re-create the intensities: the consequences are too awful, too final, and too damaging.

Still, the seductiveness of these unbridled and intense moods is powerful; and the ancient dialogue between reason and the senses is almost always more interestingly and passionately resolved in favor of the senses. The milder manias have a way of promising—and, for a very brief while, delivering—springs in the winter and epochal vitalities. In the cold light of day, however, the reality and destructiveness of rekindled illness tend to dampen the evocativeness of such selectively remembered, wistful, intense, and gentle moments. Any temptation that I now may have to recapture such moods by altering my medication is quickly hosed down by the cold knowledge that a gentle intensity soon becomes first a frenetic one and then, finally, an uncontrolled insanity. I am too frightened that I will again become morbidly depressed or virulently manic—either of which would, in turn, rip apart every aspect of my life, relationships, and work that I find most meaningful—to seriously consider any change in my medical treatment.

Although I am basically optimistic about remaining well, I know my illness from enough different vantage points to remain rather fatalistic about the future. As a result, I know that I listen to lectures about new treatments for manic-depressive illness with far more than just a professional interest. I also know that when I am doing Grand Rounds at other hospitals, I often visit their psychiatric wards, look at their seclusion rooms and ECT suites, wander their hospital grounds, and do my own internal ratings of where I would choose to go if I had to be hospitalized. There is always a part of my mind that is preparing for the worst, and another part of my mind that believes if I prepare enough for it, the worst won't happen.

Many years of living with the cyclic upheavals of manic-depressive illness has made me more philosophical, better armed, and more able to handle the inevitable swings of mood and energy that I have opted for by taking a lower level of lithium. I agree absolutely with Eliot's Ecclesiastian belief that there is a season for everything, a time for building, and "a time for the wind to break the loosened pane." Therefore, I now move more easily with the fluctuating tides of energy, ideas, and enthusiasms that I remain so subject to. My mind still, now and again, becomes a carnival of lights, laughter, and sounds and possibilities. The laughter and exuberance and ease will, filling me, spill out and over and into others. These glinting, glorious moments will last for a while, a short season, and then move on. My high moods and hopes, having ridden briefly in the top car of the Ferris wheel will, as suddenly as they came, plummet into a black and gray and tired heap. Time will pass; these moods will pass; and I will, eventually, be myself again. But then, at some unknown time, the electrifying carnival will come back into my mind.

These comings and goings, this grace and godlessness, have become such a part of my life that the wild colors and sounds now have become less strange and less strong; and the blacks and grays that inevitably follow are, likewise, less dark and frightening. "Beneath those stars," Melville once said, "is a universe of gliding monsters." But, with time, one has encountered many of the monsters, and one is increasingly less terrified of those still to be met. Although I continue to have emergences of my old summer manias, they have been gutted not only of most of their terror, but of most of their earlier indescribable beauty and glorious rush as well: sludged by time, tempered by a long string of jading experiences, and brought to their knees by medication, they now coalesce, each July, into brief, occasionally dangerous cracklings together of black moods and high passions. And then they, too, pass. One comes out of such experiences with a more surrounding sense of death, and of life. Having heard so often, and so believably, John Donne's bell tolling softly that "Thou must die," one turns more sharply to life, with an immediacy and appreciation that would not otherwise exist.

We all build internal sea walls to keep at bay the sadnesses of life and the often overwhelming forces within our minds. In whatever way we do this—through love, work, family, faith, friends, denial, alcohol, drugs, or medication—we build these walls, stone by stone, over a lifetime. One of the most difficult problems is to construct these barriers of such a height and strength that one has a true harbor, a sanctuary away from crippling turmoil and pain, but yet low enough, and permeable enough, to let in fresh sea-water that will fend off the inevitable inclination toward brackishness. For someone with my cast of mind and mood, medication is an integral element of this wall: without it, I would be constantly beholden to the crushing movements of a mental sea; I would, unquestionably, be dead or insane.

But love is, to me, the ultimately more extraordinary part of the breakwater wall: it helps to shut out the terror and awfulness, while, at the same time, allowing in life and beauty and vitality. When I first thought about writing this book, I conceived of it as a book about moods, and an illness of moods, in the context of an individual life. As I have written it, however, it has somehow turned out to be very much a book about love as well: love as sustainer, as renewer, and as protector. After each seeming death within my mind or heart, love has returned to re-create hope and to restore life. It has, at its best, made the inherent sadness of life bearable, and its beauty manifest. It has, inexplicably and savingly, provided not only cloak but lantern for the darker seasons and grimmer weather.

I long ago abandoned the notion of a life without storms, or a world without dry and killing seasons. Life is too complicated, too constantly changing, to be anything but what it is. And I am, by nature, too mercurial to be anything but deeply wary of the grave unnaturalness involved in any attempt to exert too much control over essentially uncontrollable forces. There will always be propelling, disturbing elements, and they will be there until, as Lowell put it, the watch is taken from the wrist. It is, at the end of the day, the individual moments of restlessness, of bleakness, of strong persuasions and maddened enthusiasms, that inform one's life, change the nature and direction of one's work, and give final meaning and color to one's loves and friendships.

Epilogue

I *have often asked myself*
whether, given the choice, I would choose to have manic-
depressive illness. If lithium were not available to me, or
didn't work for me, the answer would be a simple no—and
it would be an answer laced with terror. But lithium does
work for me, and therefore I suppose I can afford to pose the
question. Strangely enough I think I would choose to have
it. It's complicated. Depression is awful beyond words or
sounds or images; I would not go through an extended one
again. It bleeds relationships through suspicion, lack of con-
fidence and self-respect, the inability to enjoy life, to walk or
talk or think normally, the exhaustion, the night terrors, the
day terrors. There is nothing good to be said for it except that
it gives you the experience of how it must be to be old, to be
old and sick, to be dying; to be slow of mind; to be lacking
in grace, polish, and coordination; to be ugly; to have no
belief in the possibilities of life, the pleasures of sex, the
exquisiteness of music, or the ability to make yourself and
others laugh.

Others imply that they know what it is like to be

depressed because they have gone through a divorce, lost a job, or broken up with someone. But these experiences carry with them feelings. Depression, instead, is flat, hollow, and unendurable. It is also tiresome. People cannot abide being around you when you are depressed. They might think that they ought to, and they might even try, but you know and they know that you are tedious beyond belief: you're irritable and paranoid and humorless and lifeless and critical and demanding and no reassurance is ever enough. You're frightened, and you're frightening, and you're "not at all like yourself but will be soon," but you know you won't.

So why would I want anything to do with this illness? Because I honestly believe that as a result of it I have felt more things, more deeply; had more experiences, more intensely; loved more, and been more loved; laughed more often for having cried more often; appreciated more the springs, for all the winters; worn death "as close as dungarees," appreciated it—and life—more; seen the finest and the most terrible in people, and slowly learned the values of caring, loyalty, and seeing things through. I have seen the breadth and depth and width of my mind and heart and seen how frail they both are, and how ultimately unknowable they both are. Depressed, I have crawled on my hands and knees in order to get across a room and have done it for month after month. But, normal or manic, I have run faster, thought faster, and loved faster than most I know. And I think much of this is related to my illness—the intensity it gives to things and the perspective it forces on me. I think it has made me test the limits of my mind (which, while wanting, is holding) and the limits of my upbringing, family, education, and friends.

The countless hypomanias, and mania itself, all have brought into my life a different level of sensing and feeling

*and thinking. Even when I have been most psychotic—
delusional, hallucinating, frenzied—I have been aware of
finding new corners in my mind and heart. Some of those
corners were incredible and beautiful and took my breath
away and made me feel as though I could die right then and
the images would sustain me. Some of them were grotesque
and ugly and I never wanted to know they were there or to
see them again. But, always, there were those new corners
and—when feeling my normal self, beholden for that self to
medicine and love—I cannot imagine becoming jaded to
life, because I know of those limitless corners, with their limitless views.*

Acknowledgments

Writing a book of this kind would have been impossible without the support and advice of my friends, family, and colleagues. Certainly it would have been impossible without the excellent medical care I have received over the years from Dr. Daniel Auerbach; he has been, in every way, an excellent and deeply compassionate doctor. I owe him not only my life, but an important part of my education as a clinician as well.

No one has been more influential in my decision to be open about my manic-depressive illness than Frances Lear, a longtime friend and generous supporter of my work. She has encouraged and made possible my mental health advocacy work and is, in many significant respects, responsible for my decision to write this book. Her support and belief in my work have made a critical difference in what I have been able to do during the past eight years.

Several other friends have been particularly important. I am deeply indebted to David Mahoney for his support, many long and helpful conversations, and marvelous friendship. Dr. Anthony Storr has been one of the most important people in my life, and I am very grateful to him for our relationship. Lucie Bryant and Dr. Jeremy Waletzky, both close friends for many years, have been unbelievably kind and generous with their support. John

Julius Norwich has, for some time, encouraged me to discuss my manic-depressive illness more openly, and repeatedly stressed his belief that good will come from writing such a book; he has countered all of my arguments for privacy with yet stronger ones for straightforwardness. He has been a wonderful friend, and I am indebted to him for his persuasiveness. Peter Sacks, a poet and professor of English at Johns Hopkins, read over all of the drafts of this book, made many invaluable suggestions, and gave me much needed encouragement. I cannot thank him enough for the time and care he took with my work. Many other people have provided friendship over the years, and several of them were kind enough to read early drafts of my manuscript as well: Dr. and Mrs. James Ballenger, Dr. Samuel Barondes, Robert Boorstin, Dr. Harriet Braiker, Dr. Raymond De Paulo, Antonello and Christina Fanna, Dr. Ellen Frank, Dr. and Mrs. Robert Gallo, Dr. Robert Gerner, Dr. Michael Gitlin, Mrs. Katharine Graham, Congressman and Mrs. Steny Hoyer, Charles and Gwenda Hyman, Earl and Helen Kindle, Dr. Athanasio Koukopoulos, Dr. David Kupfer, Alan and Hannah Pakula, Dr. Barbara Parry, Dr. and Mrs. Robert Post, Victor and Harriet Potik, Dr. Norman Rosenthal, William Safire, Stephen E. Smith, Jr., Dr. Paula Stoessel, Dr. Per Vestergaard, Dr. and Mrs. James Watson, and Professor Robert Winter.

During very difficult times in Los Angeles, Dr. Robert Faguet was an extraordinary friend; as I have written, he looked after me during my absolute darkest days, and he did so with great grace and wit. My former husband, Alain Moreau, also was remarkably kind and loyal during those days, and I am grateful to him for our continuing and close relationship. Drs. Frederick

Silvers, Gabrielle Carlson, and Regina Pally in quite different ways helped keep me going during those long, terrible months. Later, when David Laurie died, several people in England were exceptionally kind, and they have remained friends over the years: Colonel and Mrs. Anthony Darlington, Colonel James B. Henderson, the late Brigadier Donald Stewart, his wife, Margaret, and Ian and Christine Mill.

The chairman of my department at Johns Hopkins, Dr. Paul McHugh, has been singularly supportive, as was, earlier, Dr. Louis Jolyon West, chairman of psychiatry during the time I was on the medical school faculty at the University of California, Los Angeles. I will always owe a great personal as well as intellectual debt to the two men who were my mentors when I was an undergraduate and graduate student, Professors Andrew L. Comrey and the late William H. McGlothlin. I have learned more than I can say, or adequately acknowledge, from both my students and my patients.

I, like many others, was devastated by the death in 1994 of publisher Erwin Glikes. He was not only a remarkable intellect and a profoundly wise human being, he was also a close friend. He published my book *Touched with Fire,* and I found it virtually impossible to imagine entrusting something as personal as these memoirs to anyone else. Fortunately, I was able to work with Carol Janeway at Knopf. She has been everything one could wish for in an editor: deeply intuitive, extremely intelligent, witty, and unrelenting in her determination to make the book a more complete and better one. It has been a pleasure and privilege to work with her. Dan Frank, the excellent editor of *Chaos,* lent his formidable editing abilities to a somewhat different kind of chaos, and helped give structure to this book. Working with the staff at Knopf has been delightful. Maxine Groffsky has been a wonderful literary agent— warm, lively, engaged, perceptive, supportive—and I am grateful that Erwin Glikes introduced us.

I am indebted to Oxford University Press for granting me permission to use material that I had written first for teaching purposes, and then incorporated—as a few brief clinical description passages—into a book I coauthored with Dr. Frederick Goodwin, *Manic-Depressive Illness.* Mr. William Collins, who typed my manuscript, was invaluably accurate, reliable, pleasant, and intelligent.

I have discussed my family at some length in this book. All meaningful relationships are complicated, but I cannot imagine choosing any family other than the one I have: my mother, Dell Temple Jamison; my father, Dr. Marshall Jamison; my brother, Dr. Dean Jamison; my sisters, Phyllis, Danica, and Kelda; my sister-in-law, Dr. Joanne Leslie; my nephews, Julian and Eliot Jamison; and my niece, Leslie Jamison.

My debt to my husband, Dr. Richard Wyatt, is beyond words. He encouraged me to write this book, supported me through all of my doubts and anxieties about doing so, read each draft of my manuscript, and made many helpful suggestions that I took to heart. I am grateful to him for a love that has endured, grown, and been wonderful.